THE STAGECRAFT
OF
BRIAN FRIEL

David Grant

Greenwich Exchange, London

First published in Great Britain in 2004
All rights reserved

The Stagecraft of Brian Friel
© David Grant 2004

Printed and bound by Q3 Digital/Litho, Loughborough
Tel: 01509 213456
Typesetting and layout by Albion Associates, London
Tel: 020 8852 4646
Cover design by December Publications, Belfast
Tel: 028 90286559

Cover photograph © Tom Lawlor, Photographer, Dublin

Greenwich Exchange Website: www.greenex.co.uk

ISBN 1-871551-74-9

for Eamon

Contents

Chronology

1920 The Government of Ireland Act 1920 allows for the creation of two self-governing units, one based on six counties of north-east Ireland (Northern Ireland) the other based on the remaining 26 counties.

1929 Brian Friel born near Omagh, Co. Tyrone, Northern Ireland.

The Censorship of Publications Act (Free State, 16th July) sets up the Irish Censorship Board; information on contraception being classified as "indecent literature".

1931 Frank O'Connor's story collection *Guests of the Nation* is published.

1932 Northern Ireland Government moves to new buildings at Stormont which are opened by Edward, Prince of Wales; the General Election in the Free State sees Eamon de Valera as Taoiseach of the first Fianna Fáil government in the Dáil (Irish Parliament); over a million people gather for mass in the Phoenix Park, Dublin – the high point of the Eucharistic Congress (22nd-26th June).

1934 Lord Craigavon, Prime Minister of Northern Ireland, makes his famous 'Protestant Nation' speech.

1935 Sean O'Casey's 'blasphemous' play, *The Silver Tassie,* provokes riots at the Abbey Theatre.

1936 The year in which *Dancing at Lughnasa* is set.

The Irish government takes a neutral stance on the Spanish Civil War; Irish volunteers go to Spain to fight on both sides; Eugene O'Neill is awarded the Nobel Prize for Literature.

1937 Fictional wedding of Maire and S.B. O'Donnell (Gar's parents in *Philadelphia, Here I Come!)*

Bunreacht na hÉireann (the Irish Constitution) is approved in a referendum. The Constitution claims sovereignty over the whole of the island of Ireland. "All powers of government, legislative, executive and judicial, derive, under God, from the people ..."

1939   The Friel family moves to Derry where Friel attends Saint Columb's College.

1945-8   Friel attends Saint Patrick's College, Maynooth; he receives a BA degree.

1948   The British government turns down a request from the government of Northern Ireland to change Northern Ireland's name to 'Ulster'.

1949   Republic of Ireland is established.

1950   Friel takes up his first teaching post in Derry, Northern Ireland.

1951   The Arts Council is founded in the Republic (8th May). The Abbey Theatre, Dublin is destroyed by fire (18th July)

1951-52   Friel writes *The Francophile*; his first essay appears in *Irish Monthly*; his first short story is published in *The Bell*.

1954   Friel marries Anne Morrison.

1955   The Republic of Ireland joins the United Nations.

1957   Alan Simpson, co-director of Tennessee Williams' *The Rose Tattoo* at the Pike Theatre, Dublin, is arrested under the obscenity laws and jailed overnight because a condom appeared on stage.

1958   *A Sort of Freedom* and *To This Hard House* broadcast on BBC Radio. *The Francophile* accepted by the Group Theatre, Belfast.

1959   Friel's short stories begin appearing in the *New Yorker*.

1960   *The Francophile* is staged at the Group Theatre.

Friel retires from teaching to become a full-time writer.

1962   *The Enemy Within* staged at the Queen's Theatre (the temporary home of the Abbey); *A Saucer of Larks* (collection of short stories published); *A Doubtful Paradise* (adapted from *The Francophile*) is broadcast on BBC Radio.

1963   *The Blind Mice* is produced at the Eblana Theatre, Dublin; Friel works with Tyrone Guthrie in Minneapolis.

1964   *Philadelphia, Here I Come!* staged at the Gaiety Theatre, Dublin as part of the Dublin Theatre Festival.

Brendan Behan's funeral is the largest to Glasnevin cemetery since that of Michael Collins.

1966   *Philadelphia, Here I Come!* runs on Broadway for six months; *The Gold in the Sea* (collection of short stories) is published. The new Abbey Theatre opens (18th July)

1967   *The Loves of Cass Maguire* is staged at the Helen Hayes Theater, New York and at the new Abbey Theatre; *Lovers* is staged at the Gate Theatre, Dublin.

The Northern Ireland Civil Rights Association (NICRA) and the Derry Housing Action Committee (DHAC) are formed.

1968   *Lovers* has its first New York production at the Lincoln Center; *Crystal and Fox* is staged at the Gaiety Theatre, Dublin.

First Civil Rights marches in Northern Ireland, commencing 24th August with a march from Coalisland to Dungannon; Northern Ireland's second university – the New University of Ulster – opens in Coleraine on 1st October, Derry/ Londonderry having been contentiously overlooked; police and Civil Rights marchers clash in Derry/Londonderry on 5th October; many marchers are injured.

1969   Friel moves with his family from Derry to the Inishowen peninsula of Donegal; *The Mundy Scheme* is rejected by the Abbey and staged at the Olympia Theatre, Dublin.

A People's Democracy march from Belfast to Derry/ Londonderry is attacked by loyalists at Burntollet Bridge on 4th January; hundreds are injured. Samuel Beckett is awarded the Nobel Prize for Literature.

1970   The year in which *The Freedom of the City* is set.

The film adaptation of *Philadelphia, Here I Come!* is released.

1971   *The Gentle Island* is staged at the Olympia Theatre, Dublin.

Internment without trial is introduced in Northern Ireland; 17 people are killed amid rioting; thousands of Catholics flee Northern Ireland to the Republic and are housed in army camps; the Ulster Defence Association emerges in Belfast in August; Sir Tyrone Guthrie dies.

1972   'Bloody Sunday' in Derry/Londonderry: 13 civilian marchers are shot dead by paratroopers on 30th January; the Stormont parliament and government are suspended on 24th March; direct rule from London is introduced; 'Bloody Friday' in Belfast (21st July): the Provisional IRA kills 19 and injures 130 in 22 bomb attacks; in 'Operation Motorman', British troops enter 'no-go' areas of Belfast and Derry/Londonderry on 30th July. In all, 467 people die in Northern Ireland violence.

Referendums in the Republic lower the voting age to 18 and remove the 'special position' of the Catholic Church from the constitution.

1973   *The Freedom of the City* is staged separately at the Abbey and the Royal Court Theatre, London; first New York production of *Crystal and Fox*.

General election for a Northern Ireland 'power-sharing' Assembly.

1974   The Ulster Workers' Council declares a general strike on 14th May: Unionist members of the executive resign on 28th May; direct rule is re-imposed the following day and the strike is called off. Power-sharing is dead.

1975   *Volunteers* is staged at the Abbey Theatre.

1977   *Living Quarters* staged at the Abbey Theatre. Controversy arises over the development by Dublin Corporation of an important Viking site at Wood Quay.

1979   *Aristocrats* is staged at the Abbey Theatre; *Faith Healer* is staged at the Colonial Theatre, Boston before opening on Broadway where it closes after a week.

Pope John Paul II visits Ireland (29th September-1st October), and celebrates mass before huge crowds in Dublin, Drogheda, Galway, Knock and Limerick; the sale and distribution of contraceptives is legalized in the Republic for 'bona fide family planning purposes'.

1980   The Field Day Theatre Company is formed by Brian Friel and Stephen Rea; *Faith Healer* is staged at the Abbey Theatre, Dublin; *Translations* is staged at the Guildhall in Derry.

Hunger strikes begin in the Maze and Armagh prisons in Northern Ireland.

1981   *Faith Healer* is staged at the Royal Court, London; first New York production of *Translations* at Manhattan Theatre Club; first London production of *Translations* at Hampstead Theatre which transfers to the National Theatre. Friel's *Three Sisters* (after Chekhov) is published by Gallery Books, Dublin.

Bobby Sands, the Provisional IRA leader in the Maze prison, begins a hunger strike on 1st March and dies on 5th May, having won a Westminster by-election in Fermanagh-South Tyrone on 9th April; nine other IRA and INLA hunger-strikers die between 10th May and 12th August; the hunger strike is called off on 3rd October.

1982   *The Communication Cord* is produced and toured by Field Day.

1983   An RTE documentary about Brian Friel and Field Day is broadcast; Friel receives an Honorary Doctorate from the National University of Ireland.

1984	Londonderry City Council votes to change its name to Derry City Council; the British government refuses permission to change the name of the city itself.
1987	Friel is appointed to the Irish Senate; *Fathers and Sons* (after Turgenev) is staged at the National Theatre, London.
1988	*Aristocrats* is staged in London and wins the Evening Standard Best Play Award; *Making History* is toured by Field Day and transfers to the National Theatre in London; Friel receives an Honorary Doctorate from the University of Ulster.
1989	*Aristocrats* is staged in New York and wins the Drama Critics Circle Award for best new foreign play; BBC Radio devotes an unprecedented six-play season to Friel.
1990	*Dancing at Lughnasa* is staged at the Abbey and transfers to the National Theatre in London.
	Mary Robinson elected President of Ireland.
1991	The Field Day Anthology of Irish Writing is published; *Dancing at Lughnasa* is named Play of the Year at the Olivier Awards in London and plays for one night in Glenties, Co. Donegal. The play also opens on Broadway to enthusiastic reviews.
1992	*Dancing at Lughnasa* receives eight Tony nominations and wins three awards including Best Play; *A Month in the Country* (after Turgenev) is staged at the Gate Theatre, Dublin; *The London Vertigo* is staged by the Gate Theatre at Andrew's Lane Theatre, Dublin.
1993	*Wonderful Tennessee* is staged at the Abbey and in New York.
1994	*Molly Sweeney* is directed by Friel himself at the Gate Theatre, Dublin and transfers to the Almeida Theatre, London; Friel resigns from Field Day.
	The IRA announces a cessation of violence (31st August); loyalist paramilitaries follow suit six weeks later (13th

October); *Riverdance* is born as an intermission item in the Eurovision Song Contest.

1995   Seamus Heaney is awarded the Nobel Prize for Literature.

1996   The first New York production of *Molly Sweeney* is directed by Friel at the Roundabout Theater and named Best Foreign Play by the New York Drama Critics Circle.

1997   *Give Me Your Answer, Do!* staged at the Abbey, directed by Friel.

1998   *Uncle Vanya* (after Chekhov) is staged at the Gate Theatre as part of the Dublin Theatre Festival. First London production of *Give Me Your Answer, Do!* at the Hampstead Theatre. Film version of *Dancing at Lughnasa* (screenplay by Frank McGuinness).

The Good Friday Agreement is negotiated by most of Northern Ireland's political parties and the British and Irish Governments (10th April) and endorsed in referendums – North (71%) and South (94%) (22nd May).

1999   The Friel Festival of eight plays (*The Freedom of the City* and *Dancing at Lughnasa* at the Abbey, *Living Quarters* and *Making History* at the Peacock, *Aristocrats* at the Gate, the Royal Shakespeare Company's production of *A Month in the Country* at the Gaiety, *Lovers* at Andrew's Lane Theatre, and *Give Me Your Answer, Do!* at the Lyric in Belfast) takes place to mark Friel's 70th birthday. An exhibition is also mounted at the National Library of Ireland; Friel receives a Lifetime Achievement Award at the *Irish Times*/ESB Theatre Awards.

2001   *The Yalta Game* is staged at the Gate Theatre for the Dublin Theatre Festival; the Abbey takes *Translations* on an international tour.

2002   *Two Plays After* (consisting of *The Bear* and *Afterplay*) are staged at the Gate Theatre; *Afterplay* goes on to the Spoleto Festival.

2003   *Performances* is staged at the Gate Theatre for the Dublin Theatre Festival.

1

A Rough Guide to Ballybeg

So you want to visit Ballybeg. You'll be wanting a guidebook, then. Here is the shop where Garreth O'Donnell grew up before emigrating to Philadelphia. Not far away is Molly Sweeney's house, and above us on the hill the battered grandeur of Ballybeg Hall, the former home of District Justice O'Donnell. There is the field where Crystal and Fox Melarkey once pitched their marquee and just outside the town, the pub where Frank Hardy, the famous faith healer, stayed and died. A short walk will take you to the remnants of the ruined farm buildings where Hugh O'Donnell held his hedge school long ago, and just beyond it is the abandoned Mundy family home.

In the four decades since Gar, the protagonist of *Philadelphia, Here I Come!*, stepped out of his father's shop and onto the stage of Dublin's Gaiety Theatre, Ballybeg in Donegal has been the home to a remarkable variety of characters and the setting for a host of plays whose stories span two centuries. Careful scrutiny of the texts will reveal all kinds of clues as to the nature of this small town, its history and its people, but its exact geography will remain elusive. Is it near Donegal town (as the play *Faith Healer* would have us believe), or up in the far north of Ireland near the present home of Ballybeg's creator, Brian Friel (as the place names in *Translations* indicate)? There is, in fact, only one effective way to travel there – on a flight of the imagination.

The critic Richard Pine has rightly observed that Ballybeg is "emblematic of all places", and this accounts for the universal impact of Friel's work from Boston to Budapest. But the secret of his wide appeal lies also in the way in which he evokes a very specific world.

As Brian Friel's good friend, Seamus Deane, has put it:

> Ballybeg has fused within it the socially depressed and
> politically dislocated world of Derry and the haunting attraction
> of the lonely landscape and traditional mores of rural Donegal.

It follows that in order fully to appreciate these plays we need to be able to fuse some understanding of the world in which the plays are set with our own personal experiences and life history.

This book is based on the premise that the best way to explore Ballybeg is to go there, and that the best way to do that is actively to explore the published plays as records of a live theatre event. To this end, Chapter 5 offers an account of actual production processes together with practical exercises aimed at facilitating an experiential engagement with three key texts. As your guide, I will draw on my experience of working closely with three of Brian Friel's best known plays, *Philadelphia, Here I Come!*, *Translations* and *Dancing at Lughnasa*. Like the author of any guidebook, therefore, the insights I share will reflect my own experiences. I hope that they will inform your own travels in the fascinating world of Brian Friel, and encourage you to make your own discoveries as you visit and revisit each of the plays. As will be seen, one of Friel's main themes is the multiplicity of ways in which we interpret and remember life. Embark on this journey, then, with an open mind, and be prepared for the unexpected as your own experience of life colours your reading and exploration of each of the plays.

As an Irish writer, Brian Friel comes from a rich narrative tradition. His first published works were short stories, and his drama has continued to display the skill of the master storyteller. Most commentators on his work concentrate on the language, themes and ideas of the plays – that is, they focus on the published text rather than on the living experience of the performance. This emphasis is understandable. Performance is, of its nature, ephemeral. The printed text is concrete, tangible, finite. Moreover, performance is an essentially subjective experience. No two members of even the same audience understand a performance in the same way. And every performance of even the same production of a play is different, influenced by a myriad of variables, most importantly the unpredictable relationship between actors and audience. To illustrate this, imagine a young person attending a performance of, say, *Philadelphia, Here I Come!*, with a relative from a different generation. The young person may well view the action from the perspective of Gar, the play's youthful protagonist. An older female relative might find herself identifying with Madge, the housekeeper. An older male might empathise with Gar's father, or Master Boyle. Each will bring their own experience to bear on their reading of the performance. The whole process is subjective.

Criticism, however, implies objectivity, and critics write with appropriate authority. My own experience of rehearsal has led me to be suspicious of such unequivocal analysis. Interpretation is necessarily subjective. Once actors take up the text and animate it, they inevitably instil it with their own understanding of the truth. And the test of this subjective truth is their ability to perform it. If it were not true for them in the moment of performance they simply could not play the parts. The subjective nature of experience is not only central to the way in which live theatre works – it is also the key to unlocking much of the work of Brian Friel.

Another difficulty with the conventional critical emphasis on the printed text is that the sheer theatricality of Friel's drama is often overlooked. If, as Seamus Deane maintains "brilliance in theatre has for Irish dramatists been linguistic" and that "formally the Irish theatrical tradition has not been highly experimental, (and) depends almost exclusively on talk", the briefest survey of Brian Friel's canon will reveal that for all his mastery of words, he is a signal exception to Deane's rule. The director, Conall Morrison, has described the dual characterisation of Garreth O'Donnell as "Public" and "Private" in *Philadelphia, Here I Come!* in 1964 as the theatrical equivalent of splitting the atom, releasing a surge of a new kind of energy onto the Dublin stage. From then, through the bi-linguality of *Translations* in 1980, right up to the strikingly unusual treatment of 'unspoken' thoughts in *The Yalta Game* in 2001, and the integration of a string quartet into the action of *Performances* in 2003, Friel has consistently been one of the most innovative theatrical thinkers in English-language and indeed world theatre. As he himself has said more than once, for him "the crux of (a) new play arises with its form". In considering his work, we must therefore attach due weight to the implications of live performance.

3

In practice, of course, form and substance are inseparable, and when we come to the content of his plays, it is inevitable that we look to his life and times to inform our understanding of them. But we should do so with a caution born of the knowledge that Friel himself is slow to embellish on what the plays themselves contain. The collection, *Essays, Diaries, Interviews 1964-1999*, edited by Christopher Murray to mark Friel's 70th birthday, is an invaluable resource, and as the theatre historian Christopher Morash has rightly observed, "there is a sense in which Friel is his own best interpreter". But these personal insights are as remarkable for their rarity as for their incisiveness. Friel is especially circumspect when it comes to the question of autobiography.

In his 'Self-Portrait', written in 1972, he reflects on his suspicion for 'facts'. He was born, he tells us in 1929 in Omagh, but even this is not as simple as it seems. To begin with, he has two birth certificates for consecutive days, the 9th and 10th of January, giving rise to his characteristically wry suggestion: "perhaps I'm twins!". Then there is the question of geography. Friel was actually born, not in Omagh, but in Killyclogher (a townland just outside it), a few miles away from the Irish border. This border, which separated his birthplace from his mother's family home in Glenties in County Donegal where he would spend many of his childhood holidays, was itself only five years older than he was. Even the most seemingly cut and dried 'facts' are open to question.

What does it mean in 1929, for instance, to say that Friel was born in 'Northern Ireland', when the state itself was in its infancy and would not yet have acquired any clear identity for those that lived within its borders. The sudden and sometimes arbitrary nature of this new arrangement has been vividly captured by the County Armagh poet, Paul Muldoon in his poem 'Boundary Commission'[1]:

> *You remember that village where the border ran*
> *Down the middle of the street,*
> *With the butcher and the baker in different states?*
> Today he remarked how a shower of rain
> Had stopped so cleanly across Golightly's Lane
> It might have been a wall of glass

That had toppled over. He stood there, for ages,
To wonder which side, if any, he should be on.

From the outset, then, Friel's was an ambiguous world. He was born amid the teething troubles of a new political order. In Dublin, then the capital of the Irish Free State, Micheal MacLiammoir and Hilton Edwards (who 35 years later would direct *Philadelphia, Here I Come!*) had just opened their production of Oscar Wilde's *Salome* at the Gate Theatre as a direct challenge to the Censorship of Publications Act, which was then before the new Irish Parliament, the Dáil. In July they would premiere Denis Johnston's mould-breaking play *The Old Lady Says No!* In Northern Ireland there was also a new Parliament, which would soon be given a monumental home at Stormont. This, David Trimble, the First Minister of Northern Ireland, would later describe as "a cold house for Catholics" during his Nobel Peace Prize speech in 1998. Friel himself would call it "either absurd or iniquitous, probably both".

When Friel was 10, his father, Patrick, who had been principal of a National Primary School near Omagh, took up a new teaching post in Derry. Apart from two and a half years at Saint Patrick's College in Maynooth, a year training to be a teacher at Saint Joseph's in Belfast, and a seminal six months in 1963 as an "observer" at Tyrone Guthrie's theatre in Minneapolis, Friel was to continue to live there until the late 1960s. When he then moved with his wife, Anne, and five children across the border to the Inishowen peninsula of Donegal he found himself in what the poet Paul Durcan has described as "that part of the South of Ireland that is more northerly than the North". What meaning have 'facts' when even compass points become a matter for interpretation! The answer may lie in Hugh Mor O'Donnell's assertion in *Translations* that "confusion is not an ignoble condition".

Although his father was closely involved in local political life and Friel himself was for a time a member of the Nationalist party, Northern Ireland was a frustrating place for a Catholic like Friel to put his faith in politics. Protestant power, even where Catholics were in the majority, was ensured by the most unscrupulous of means, and often elections were uncontested, the status quo being maintained in backroom deals. Undoubtedly Friel found in his short stories and later in his plays a more subtle instrument than politics on which to play out his ideas, and he gave up his teaching job to write full-time in 1960. But he was aware of only an intuitive knowledge of play-writing and play production, "like a painter who has never studied anatomy".

Friel has dismissed his second stage play, *The Blind Mice* (staged at the Eblana Theatre, Dublin in 1963) as "very poor" and has never allowed either it or his first play, *The Francophile* (produced by the Group Theatre, Belfast, in 1960) to be published. His third stage play and first Abbey Theatre premiere, *The Enemy Within* (1962), on the other hand, he considers to have been "a commendable sort of a play", "a solid play". The biblical title referred to the family of Saint Columba, the play's main protagonist. "You have to get away from a corrupting influence", he said of it. An invitation from Tyrone Guthrie, one of the greatest theatre directors of the 20th century, to visit him in Minneapolis and a £1,000 grant from the Arts Council gave him his own chance to get away. Apart from increasing his practical understanding of the theatre, Friel relished the sense of liberation from "inbred, claustrophobic Ireland" that his time in America gave him:

> And that sense of liberation conferred on me a valuable self-confidence and a necessary perspective so that the first play I wrote immediately after I came home, *Philadelphia, Here I Come!*, was a lot more assured than anything I had attempted before.

It would be a mistake, however, to misconstrue Friel's lack of theatrical experience as naivety. On his return to Ireland, he proved adept in negotiations with directors and producers and was successful in limiting Hilton Edwards' attempts to tamper with *Philadelphia, Here I Come!* Christopher Fitzsimons' refreshingly anecdotal and insightful biography of Edwards and his partner Micheal MacLiammoir, *The Boys*, provides a delicious insight into Friel's association with the Gate Theatre which the flamboyant pair had founded and run. Edwards, Fitzsimons tell us, had received the script of *Philadelphia, Here I Come!* from the Dublin Theatre Festival Director, Brendan Smith, because another management was having difficulty in casting it. Edwards was generous with his advice and urged Friel to relocate a bar scene to the house to maintain the continuity of the action – a suggestion which was duly adopted. But the playwright resisted the suggestion that one of the three 'Boys' be cut, and Edwards acceded to Friel's instinct that all three were essential. Confirming this in a letter to Edwards in August 1964, Friel added:

> At this stage I prefer not to think of your other suggestion that we cut the play during rehearsal by fifteen minutes. I know this is going to be a Chinese Death by 1,000 Cuts for me ... I'll face this damnation when the time arises (although I *know* now that every word of the play is vital).

His confidence was vindicated by the play's phenomenal success at the 1964 Dublin Theatre Festival, and subsequently on Broadway and in the West End. Edwards himself went on to direct Friel's next three plays: *The Loves of Cass Maguire*, (which echoed its protagonist's own story by opening in New York in 1966 before returning to Ireland at the Abbey in 1967), *Lovers* (at Dublin's Gate Theatre in 1967) and *Crystal and Fox* (at the Gaiety Theatre in 1968).

From 1969 until the late 1970s a new play by Friel was produced every two years. To begin with, this took place within the commercial environment of Dublin's Olympia Theatre (*The Mundy Scheme* in 1969 and *The Gentle Island* in 1971), but as Friel's status grew and the economics of commercial theatre became more uncertain, it was natural that the subsidised National Theatre, the Abbey, should become the regular home for his next four plays: *The Freedom of the City* in 1973, *Volunteers* in 1975, *Living Quarters* in 1977 and *Aristocrats* in 1979. 1979 also saw Friel's first New York premiere since *The Loves of Cass Maguire*, when James Mason starred in the first short-lived production of *Faith Healer*. In the same year, Friel renewed his friendship with the Belfast actor, Stephen Rea, whom he had met in the cast of the London production of *The Freedom of the City*, when it had been directed by Albert Finney at the Royal Court Theatre soon after the play's Abbey premiere in 1973. Rea, who in 1979 was playing Eamon in the premiere of *Aristocrats* took great interest in Friel's plans to open his next production in Derry. Although there is now a vibrant regional professional theatre movement throughout Ireland, at that time the very idea of a production base outside the three main cities of Dublin, Belfast and Cork was, to say the least, eccentric. But both Friel and Rea shared a desire for the arts to transcend the limitations of conventional Nationalist-Unionist politics in an effort to discover what came to be known as a 'fifth province' of the imagination. Although the original intention was for just one production, in order to secure funding from the Arts Council of Northern Ireland, it was necessary legally to incorporate a theatre company, and so the Field Day Theatre Company was born, named for its two founders, Friel and Rea.

As Irish Nationalists, both Friel and Rea were opposed to the partition of Ireland. After more than a decade of the Ulster 'Troubles', however, the failure of either the terrorists or the politicians to make progress was all too obvious. Friel has always been cautious about engaging directly with the political situation and has come to regret the urgency that made *The Freedom of the City* so overtly political a play. But it is too simplistic to say that he is apolitical. In an interview in 1986 he expressed it this way:

> The conflict between the public self, the social self and the artistic self, demands privacy, demands secrecy, demands inversion.

In a booklet published as part of his 70th birthday celebrations, he relates the Russian folk-tale about a mythical town called Kitezh:

> The story goes that when Kitezh sensed that marauders were approaching, it encased itself in a mist and shrank into it and vanished from sight. But even as it disappeared, even after it had disappeared, the church bell never stopped ringing and it could be heard through the mist and over the whole countryside … for me the true gift of theatre, the real benediction of all art, is the ringing bell which reverberates quietly and persistently in the head long after the curtain has gone down … Because until the marauders withdraw and the fog lifts, that sacred song is the only momentary stay we have against confusion.

Ballybeg is Friel's Kitezh, and Field Day Theatre Company was an attempt to intone that ringing bell. The image recalls the more prosaic symbolism of an early working title for his play *Aristocrats – The*

Canary in the Mineshaft. Like the importance of the canary to miners fearing gas, the importance of art becomes most apparent when it ceases to speak to us.

As we shall see, Field Day's "marauders" proved mainly to be a group of critics and historians, and following the inaugural production of *Translations* (1980) and Friel's version of Chekhov's *Three Sisters*, Friel's next play, *The Communication Cord*, was a conscious response to the accusations Field Day's first production had given rise to. After that, Friel fell silent as a dramatist for nearly five years and Field Day produced work by other writers. Encouraged by his wife, Anne, to find an escape route from his writer's block, he wrote an adaptation of Turgenev's *Fathers and Sons* which was produced by the National Theatre in London in 1987. This seems to have provided the stimulus needed to bring forth his next long-awaited play about Hugh O'Neill, the seventeenth-century Earl of Tyrone, *Making History*. As the clever pun of the title suggests, this was more than mere biography. As we shall see in Chapter 3, it is a detailed examination of the relationship between history and fiction and between different sorts of truth.

As well as being a rounding off of the debate that had been sparked off by *Translations*, *Making History* was also to be Friel's last play for Field Day. His decision to give his next play, the internationally successful *Dancing at Lughnasa*, to the Abbey must have generated tensions within Field Day, which would ultimately lead to his departure from the company in 1994. Although Field Day continued to produce new work, the tours became increasingly irregular, and although it was nominally co-producer of Stewart Parker's *Northern Star* with Tinderbox Theatre Company in 1998, it had by then lost both its momentum and most crucially its continuity of funding. For Friel, in any case, an experiment that had transformed the assumptions governing theatre production in Ireland and that had given rise not only to numerous important plays but also to a whole intellectual movement, had come to a natural end.

Throughout the 1990s Friel's principal collaborator was to be the producer, Noel Pearson, who ensured the international exploitation of *Dancing at Lughnasa*, and produced its successor, *Wonderful Tennessee* in Dublin and on Broadway. All his subsequent plays and adaptations to date, apart from *Give Me Your Answer, Do!* Other than *Give Me Your Answer, Do!* at the Abbey in 1997, all his subsequent plays and adaptations to date have been produced by Michael Colgan, the successor of MacLiammoir and Edwards at the Gate Theatre (*The London Vertigo* in 1991, *A Month in the Country* in 1992, *The Yalta Game* in 2001 and *Performances* in 2003).

Friel's spectacular return to the centre of Irish theatre production, has been matched by an impressive series of tributes and accolades. As early as 1983 he received an Honorary Doctorate from the National University of Ireland (the Irish equivalent of a knighthood), followed by similar awards from the University of Ulster, Queen's University, Belfast, Trinity College, Dublin and the Dublin City University. In 1989, in his 60th year, BBC radio produced a season of no less than six of his plays. In the same year he received the *Sunday Independent/ Irish Life* Arts Award for Theatre; and a decade later a grand total of eight plays (seven in Dublin and one in Belfast) were produced to mark his 70th birthday. He also received a Lifetime Achievement Award in the 1999 ESB/*Irish Times* Theatre Awards. It is traditional in Ireland to celebrate dead playwrights. The pictures of Sheridan, Goldsmith, Wilde, Shaw, Synge, O'Casey, Beckett and Behan are to be found in almost every pub on the island. But it is rare for such recognition to be extended to a writer in his own lifetime.

Footnotes
[1] Paul Muldoon, *Selected Poems 1968-1983* (Faber, London, 1986) p.48.

2

History

The idea that there is no such thing as absolute truth, but only competing versions of the truth, is at the heart of much of Brian Friel's drama. It is a theme which establishes itself firmly in *Philadelphia, Here I Come!*, recurs in *The Loves of Cass Maguire* and *The Freedom of the City*, is pathologised in *Living Quarters*, codified in *Making History*, and reaches its most assured form in *Faith Healer*. This idea is also central to an understanding of how we present and perceive plays. Live drama is an essentially subjective phenomenon, because life is subjective. However scientific our sensibilities may be, however much we aspire to the certainties of objectivity, the governing reality is the individuality of each person's experience. This is how drama works.

As we saw in the last chapter, when we sit in a theatre, no matter how many other individuals are sitting there with us, our perception of what is taking place before us will be unique. Our relationship with the characters will be influenced by the associations we make between them and people in our own lives and by the perspective we bring to the action. We will tend to empathise with characters of our own age or gender. We will tend to interpret the play through their eyes. *An Phoblacht*, the republican newspaper, for instance, viewed the minor character of Doalty in Friel's *Translations* to be at the heart of the play, presumably identifying with his commitment to fighting back against the English.

Even our location in the theatre will affect the way in which we engage with the drama. If we are close to the stage we may respond more to the intensity of the performance. If we are further back we may be more aware of the overall shape of the production. Whereas in a cinematic spectacle the editor and director guide our eye, in the theatre, even though lighting can focus our attention, we become our own editor and director. The play, then, does not take shape on the stage, but in the mind of each of the spectators. In an audience of 300, there are, in fact, 300 versions of the play. And when we leave the theatre, and discuss with others what each of us has seen, we will discover differences of detail, emphasis and interpretation. We will remember different versions of the truth.

It is perhaps for this reason that Brian Friel comments on his work so rarely. For him, the plays must stand for themselves, without extraneous annotation, and we should be wary when we refer to his occasional articles, interviews and 'sporadic diaries' of interposing yet another layer of interpretation. And yet, when Friel, mindful of the risk he takes, tantalisingly offers us a 'Self-Portrait', the sense that he is giving us a key to his craft is irresistible. The date is 1972. There have been five more plays since the success of *Philadelphia, Here I Come!* in 1964, and Friel allows himself some respite for reflection. And immediately he finds himself wrestling with the impossibility of autobiography. In particular, he is troubled by the tension between fact and fiction.

By way of example he remembers, in exquisite detail, a fishing expedition with his father when he was about nine years old – "a particular memory of a particular day". But for all the vividness of the memory he is "conscious of a dissonance, an unease … there is no lake along that muddy road … The fact is fiction … For some reason, the mind has shuffled the pieces of veritable truth and composed a truth of its own". The process by which he then "acknowledges its peculiar veracity" and makes it part of himself, provides the perfect metaphor for his facility as a dramatist. In his 1975 play, *Volunteers*, Friel explicitly explores the symbolism inherent in archaeology, as layers of history are scraped away revealing "a tangible précis of the story of Irish man". But throughout his work, Friel is consciously excavating what in 'Self-Portrait' he describes as his own "subsoil", intuitively blending insight and experience into a re-imagined reality. So when at the end of the 'Self-Portrait' Friel tells us he assumes that we will look "beyond the innocent outspread hands", he licenses us to probe the plays and unearth our own discoveries there.

Those familiar with *Philadelphia, Here I Come!*, will immediately recognise the story of the fishing trip as the inspiration for Gar's most precious memory of his father. But whereas Friel has become reconciled to the vagaries of recollection, for Gar the treachery of his own memory propels him into exile. If asked to say briefly what the play is about, you might explain that it is an account of a young Donegal man's last night at home before emigrating to America. You might catalogue the other characters: his father, S.B. O'Donnell, shop keeper and councillor; Madge, the faithful housekeeper; Canon Mick O'Byrne, his father's friend; and the other visitors to the house that night – "the boys", his sad old schoolmaster, and Kate Doogan, the girl he failed to woo. You would comment on the use of flashback to convey the visit of his American aunt and her entourage, and you would certainly allude to the device that most distinguishes the play – the stage presence of Gar's private thoughts embodied by a second actor. All these things are vital to a circumstantial understanding of the play. But its essence lies in its manipulation of different forms of truth and how this hampers the communication of what Friel will later (in *Translations*) describe as "privacies" and "the private core".

The shattering of the precious memories that Gar has cherished from childhood (the blue boat, the rain, the singing of 'All Around my Hat') has such dramatic power because the audience have been allowed access to his inner core through the presence on stage of Private Gar. They know the full extent of his pain, and the way in which this one memory has come to symbolise Gar's whole relationship with his father. He has made a heavy emotional investment in it, and when it fails his whole sense of belonging in Ballybeg crashes down with it. But the explicit representation of Gar's private thoughts serves another important dramatic function. It attunes the audience's sensitivity to the unspoken thoughts of the whole cast. Subtly to reveal such subtext is the goal of every actor. And *Philadelphia, Here I Come!*, by making thought flesh, provides a heightened environment in which to realise this aim.

The other characters, of course, have to reveal themselves in more conventional ways. The duplicity of "the boys", with their misrepresentation of bullying as bravado, is transparent enough. Kate's evasion of the truth is more benign. Master Boyle clings to dubious memories of Gar having sent him cigarettes and jam, which if true, have clearly not retained the same significance for Gar. Most poignantly, his father nurtures his own memory of Gar, in a "wee sailor suit" at home from school and wanting to take over the shop – a fantasy immediately exploded by Madge, in whose knowledge of Gar's wardrobe the audience are inclined to place more trust. All these constructed memories reflect the 'facts' as the characters might have liked them to have been – the Master's memory of a devoted pupil, the father's desire for a dutiful son, the son's craving for a caring father.

Gar's mantra provides a clue to this. Throughout the play, in moments of distraction, he resorts to the incantation of the opening lines from the 18th-century Anglo-Irish orator and politician, Edmund Burke's *Reflections on the Revolution in France*. This is usually interpreted as reflecting Burke's own desire to mythologise the French monarchy in pursuit of his own counter-revolutionary agenda. Just as Burke manufactures a romanticised version of the truth to suit his own purposes, so Gar and other characters in the play distort the truth to their own ends. The irony is that the mysterious power of the frequent repetition of this passage by Gar in the play has generated its own mythology. One actor with whom I have worked, whose father was at school with Friel, was adamant that it derived from Friel's own experience of a schoolmaster who used Burke's words in a similar way. Another reported asking Friel outright the significance of the passage only to be told that Friel shared her curiosity. That this fantasised vision of Queen Marie Antoinette is so often linked in Gar's mind with the women who haunt his thoughts (Kate and his long-dead mother) is clearly not coincidental. But in the end, the only real theatrical truth is that it works supremely well on stage.

Ultimately, the power of the play is to show what the characters' dialogue alone cannot reveal, most tellingly in the silent scene in which Gar's father, S.B. O'Donnell, approaches his son's bedroom door and hesitates in front of it, before finally turning away. The love that a good actor can convey through that shuffling walk outweighs all his words. The failure of communication runs through the play and is never more obvious than in the character of S.B. When, following its triumphant reception at the 1964 Dublin Theatre Festival, plans were laid for a production of the play on Broadway, the company were obliged by the rules of American Equity, the actors' union, to justify the retention of Irish actors for the New York run. The centrality of the roles of Private and Public Gar were acknowledged, and Madge was conceded to have a substantial part. But on paper, S.B.'s contribution did not pass muster. He had too few lines to be so crucial to the production that he could not be replaced with an American actor. Eventually, however, the original actor was allowed to perform in New York when it seems to have been accepted that it was what he *didn't* say that made him so indispensable to the play.

Despite the radical device of dividing his central character between two actors and the use of flashback, *Philadelphia, Here I Come!*, appears to conform to the prevailing naturalism of most Irish Theatre. Its closest model is perhaps a memory play such as Arthur Miller's *Death of a Salesman*. But even that analogy hints at the play's more complex form. Miller originally called his own play *The Inside of His Skull*. Like Gar in *Philadelphia, Here I Come!*, Miller's salesman, Willy Loman, brings the audience into the world of his own memory and imagination, jumping in time and place. In a similar way, the critic, Anthony Roche, sees the key to understanding *Philadelphia, Here I Come!* in Gar's final image of the night's events as a film which he "will run over and over again" in his imagination. He suggests that the play's apparent present is perhaps actually the past as rehearsed in Gar's subsequent memory, and finds a parallel device in Beckett's *Krapp's Last Tape* where the eponymous Krapp replays tapes of his former life. The notion is an enticing one, especially given the importance accorded in the play to the interpretation of memory, but it cannot entirely explain the play's structure. Although Gar allows us access to the visit of his aunt and his encounter with Kate's father in flashback, there are important scenes between Madge and S.B. which lose their dramatic force if they are understood by the audience to be mere projections of Gar's imagination. It is precisely because they contradict Gar's prejudices that they are so powerful. I prefer to see *Philadelphia, Here I Come!* as one of a lifelong series of experiments in which Brian Friel has continued to explore the diverse possibilities of live drama, imposing his own unique logic in the specific case of each successive play.

Friel's next experiment, *The Loves of Cass Maguire,* was premiered at the Helen Hayes Theater in New York in 1966. It provides a natural complement to *Philadelphia, Here I Come!*, addressing as it does the home-coming of an exile, returning from America after more than fifty years. The two plays also inhabit the same stylistic sphere, with many of the scenes being channelled through the memory and imagination of the central character. But Friel is even bolder in *The Loves of Cass Maguire*. In *Philadelphia, Here I Come!* he offers clear advice about the playing of the two Gars. Private can see Public, but not vice versa. "One cannot look at one's alter-ego". In *The Loves of Cass Maguire* he goes further. "Cass," he instructs, "directly addresses the audience. They are her friends, her intimates. The other people on stage are interlopers". Thus Friel challenges the unspoken conventions that traditionally govern the relationship between audience and actors. The play opens uncontroversially with a domestic scene. Then suddenly Cass "charges on stage (either from the wings or from the auditorium)". The very fact that the option is offered to break through realism's 'fourth wall' sets the tone for the rest of the play. "Cass, you can't break in … ", her brother Harry exclaims. The line fulfils a naturalistic function in the scene, but he could just as easily be talking about her disruption of the theatrical norm.

The approach is hardly revolutionary. Friel's mentor, Tyrone Guthrie, had spent a lifetime seeking to free theatre from the constraints of the proscenium arch, and *Our Town* by Thornton Wilder (a playwright Friel admires) had irreparably broken all the rules as early as 1938, establishing with his stage manager character a beachhead for Brechtian principles on the English-speaking stage. But what makes Friel's approach in *The Loves of Cass Maguire* so intriguing is that the play's meta-theatricality becomes part of the psyche of Cass herself. It is as if the discomfort of the audience at the play's intrusiveness connects them with the character's own sense of dislocation and unease. It seeks to conform to naturalistic principles, even when it seems to struggle most against them. In this way, Cass's ability directly to address the audience becomes a form of madness, which only leaves her when she acquires the capacity to live out an internal fantasy, in common with the other inhabitants of Eden House, an old people's home. Her plight recalls the H.G Wells short story, 'The Kingdom of the Blind', in which a one-eyed man finds himself in a community where nobody can see and his residual vision is treated as a form of insanity. (Friel's own once blind Molly Sweeney also comes to mind.)

Cass's unique vision is of her place within her own story. "*The Loves of Cass Maguire*. Where did he get that title anyway," she says, presumably referring to Friel. And slowly the audience begins to doubt the reality of what they see on stage. Is it real, we ask, or is it in Cass's memory? And Friel makes the audience Cass's principle bulwark against the things she would prefer to forget, allowing her to retain contact with us while characters intrude into the shadowy background of her consciousness. Eden House offers her an apprenticeship in self-delusion and she becomes fascinated by the antics of Trilbe, a fellow resident, who inhabits her own sort of celtic twilight. In one scene Friel indicates that Trilbe plays "on two levels at once: she is her normal, vital self ... and at the same time she must convey the first inklings of otherness, of the private world she ... take(s) refuge in occasionally." "Join with us, Catherine," she urges Cass, "for we have the truth ... We know what is real." This is a world where artificial flowers are preferable to real ones, and where Cass becomes bewitched by the healing power of pretence, much as Hamlet is astounded at the capacity of the Player King to give "all for Hecuba".

The play's reflexive self-awareness of its own theatricality is reminiscent of Pirandello (another acknowledged influence on Friel). To an even greater extent than *Philadelphia, Here I Come!* the play derives its fluidity from the seamless shifts from scene to scene that this approach allows. But in the end, the play's bold form seems to explain itself away, as Cass relinquishes the lifeline of audience contact to Eden House's next bewildered newcomer.

Friel continued to experiment with form in his next double-barrelled play, *Lovers* (1967), counterpointing the optimism of the young Mag and Joe in 'Winners' (the first half) with the frustration and disillusionment of the older Andy and Hanna in 'Losers' (the second half). He links the plays by having the actors who play the older couple punctuate the action of the first play with a neutral commentary revealing to the audience that Mag and Joe will die in a drowning accident immediately following the scene we share with them. They are winners in Friel's view presumably because their youthful hopes are not destroyed by the bitterness of having to live through them. The critic, Michael Billington, found this device "maudlin", but it can achieve great poignancy in performance. More importantly, the use of detached commentators represents another experiment on Friel's part in the management of his audience. In 'Losers', he exploits the comic potential of having a character directly address the audience, by allowing Andy to keep stepping out of the action in order to share with us an account of his love life with the bitter and subdued Hanna. There is no attempt at Brechtian distance here. Rather an extended use of the traditional 'aside'.

Friel's next two plays, *Crystal & Fox* (1968) and *The Gentle Island* (1971), each present us with marginalised communities clinging to dying traditions in which an older generation is at odds with the young – a fusion of the two components of *Lovers* with predictably explosive results. The former play is chiefly memorable for its excursion into the literal world of theatre, and opens with a backstage view of a ramshackle performance in which "the unseen audience is restless and not very respectful; they have long since grown tired of suspending their disbelief." It is as if Friel, having tested the boundaries of theatre convention in the various ways outlined above now wants to engage with the idea of theatre itself. To this extent, the play is a prototype for the much more successful *Faith Healer* more than a decade later. *The Gentle Island* is set on Inishkeen, which as well as being an Irish translation of the play's title, also carries the meaning 'Island of Lament'. This ambiguity parallels the representation of Manus, the island's self-styled 'king', whose latent savagery cannot be disguised beneath a veil of storytelling and lore. When outsiders visit the island, the shallowness of this mythology is exposed and Manus exacts a terrible revenge.

Like Friel's earlier plays, *The Gentle Island* and *Crystal and Fox* both present us with conflicting versions of the truth, in each case with highly destructive results. But these distortions inform the drama rather than govern it. In his next play, *The Freedom of the City* (1973), the representation of 'the facts' again becomes the idea on which the drama turns. Produced at the Abbey Theatre, the year after the now notorious events of Bloody Sunday when 13 unarmed civilians were shot dead by British soldiers following an illegal Civil Rights demonstration in Derry city, *The Freedom of the City* echoes many aspects of those events and the Widgery Tribunal that followed them.

In an interview with Eavan Boland (1973) Friel was adamant: "It's not about Bloody Sunday. In fact, the play began long before Bloody Sunday happened". But in 1982 in an interview with Fintan O'Toole he was more circumspect, observing that "one of the problems with that play was that the experience of Bloody Sunday wasn't adequately distilled in me."

Reaching the Abbey at a time when memories of the killings were still so raw, the play was bound to excite controversy, and was widely perceived as partisan and anti-British. But a recent revival by the director, Conall Morrison, placing greater emphasis on what, according to Morrison was a deliberate experiment by Friel with Brechtian techniques, has allowed for a better understanding of its complex structure, the seeds of which can be seen in his earlier work. In *The Freedom of the City*, Friel expands the role of the external commentator with which he experimented in 'Winners' into a full-scale inquiry with multiple witnesses including a policeman, a sociologist, a priest, a pathologist and a brigadier and also adds the perspectives of a television journalist, an army press officer and a balladeer. The accounts of these witnesses frame the central action in which three hapless refugees from the riot that follows a Civil Rights demonstration find themselves in Derry's Guildhall – the symbol of Unionist power. They are ultimately shot dead by British soldiers when they attempt to surrender. From the outset, the commentators contradict the facts as the audience can see them, with the journalist declaring "unconfirmed reports of about 50 armed gunmen", the army press officer referring to "a band of terrorists … [of] up to 40 persons", and the balladeer with Falstaffian hyperbole conjuring up the image of "a 100 Irish heroes".

Viewed with hindsight, it is easier to appreciate Friel's wider intentions for the play, which began, under the working title of *John Butt's Bothy,* as an exploration of 18th-century poverty during the period of widespread evictions of peasants from their land. The events of Bloody Sunday undoubtedly served as a powerful catalyst for these emerging ideas, but it is easy to see the social concerns that remain at the play's centre. Amid all the rhetoric and officialese, Friel presents three individuals, each with an engaging story to tell. Michael is the idealist, who sees the Civil Rights movement as a means of bettering himself and who relishes the way in which it levels social difference, "rich and poor, high and low, doctors, accountants, plumbers, teachers, bricklayers – all shoulder to shoulder". Skinner is the cynic, preoccupied with his own survival. Lily is a kind of Everywoman, older than the others, and the vehicle for Friel's searing exposition of the day-to-day reality of abject poverty.

As in *The Loves of Cass Maguire* and in 'Winners', Friel exploits the dramatist's power to deconstruct chronology, not only giving the audience privileged information which the characters within the action do not share, but also indicating connections between the play's outer shell (the tribunal) and its inner core (the three protagonists). Most tellingly, he extends the technique by which Cass was permitted direct access to the audience by allowing Michael, Skinner and Lily to speak beyond the grave, and in doing so he imbues them with a clarity and simplicity of language and delivery, which assumes a greater authority than all the posturing of the various external witnesses. The effect is particularly effective in the case of Lily, who is freed by the magic of theatre from a lifetime of educational and social disadvantage, into a new expressiveness.

By placing these testimonies at the beginning of Act Two he colours the audience's perception of all that follows. Furthermore, by delaying the moment at which the audience sees the actual circumstances of the victims' death until the final moments of the play, (that is, after the findings of the Tribunal have been revealed), he implicates the whole panoply of commentators in their deaths, highlighting (as the theatre historian Lionel Pilkington astutely observes) "the inevitable and universal complicity between the state and all forms of representation".

Friel revisits this sense of the individual as the victim of a constructed history in his next play, *Volunteers* (1975). A group of Republican internees (prisoners detained without trial) have 'volunteered' to assist with an archaeological dig. Unlike *The Freedom of the City*, the form appears to be entirely naturalistic, but again Friel privileges the audience with information known only to them and to the prisoners by revealing at the end of the First Act that all of the 'volunteers' are to be murdered in a staged riot when they return to jail. This serves to heighten the audience's reading of the contrast between the honest enthusiasm of the prisoners in the search for archaeological truth and the cynicism of the professor who seems interested only in gathering enough material for his next book. When one of the prisoners challenges the validity of some of the professor's conclusions by pointing to inconsistencies in the evidence, he is met with embarrassed silence. Meanwhile, the prisoners take refuge in "the protection of the myth" by spinning story after story around the unearthed Viking skeleton of 'Lief', himself apparently a murder victim.

What links *The Freedom of the City* and *Volunteers* is not so much their shared political context, as the tension they reveal between official and individual versions of the truth. Towards the end of *Volunteers*, one of the prisoners is asked to stand in a photograph of the excavation "to give the picture a scale". This sense of the individual only having a relevance in the context of a wider purpose echoes the plight of the central characters in *The Freedom of the City*. What arguably makes *Volunteers* the more successful play, is that Friel is true to his own theatrical instinct, informed, as we have seen, by years of experimental practice. Rather than a clinical Brechtianism, we see a return to the core device of *Philadelphia, Here I Come!* in the creation of the inspired double-act of Pyne and Keeney whose ceaseless banter articulates the private dimension of the play. Friel adapts the highly stylised technique evident in Private Gar to a naturalistic convention, while retaining the heightened energy of the earlier character. Indeed, with reference to both *Freedom of the City* and *Volunteers* as a whole, it is helpful to equate the distinction used above between official and individual with the broader notions of 'public' and 'private'.

By the time we come to Friel's next stage play, *Living Quarters* (1977) there is a distinct sense of him reviewing his stagecraft, and using this play to express his findings. Taking his character structure from Euripides' *Hippolytus*, Theseus becomes Commandant Frank Butler, recently returned from distinguished service for the United Nations as part of the Irish army, Phaedra becomes his new young wife Anna, and his son Ben stands for an unlikely Hippolytus. In place of Olympus, Friel creates 'Sir' in his own image, part playwright/part narrator/part God. The play opens with Sir's exposition of theatre as a therapeutic ritual, remarkable in the light of the above consideration of Friel's developing inventiveness as a dramatist. Speaking of the crucial day that is to be the subject of the drama, he explains:

> … the people who were involved in the events of that day, although they're now scattered all over the world, every so often in sudden moments of privacy, of isolation, of panic, they remember that day, and in their imagination they reconvene here to reconstruct it – what was said, what was not said, what was done, what was not done, what might have been said, what might have been done; endlessly raking over those dead episodes that can't be left at peace.

The speech recalls Gar's closing 'camera' speech in *Philadelphia, Here I Come!* and also brings to mind Arthur Miller's dictum: "when I show you why a man does what he does, I may do so melodramatically; but when I show why he almost did not do it, I am making drama". Sir's role has undoubtedly many parallels with that of the dramatist. He maps out the journey that each character must take, mindful of "the memory of those lost possibilities" that have haunted them. He is inclined to do so chronologically, but finds them rebelling, however ineffectually, against him. The role of Sir provides a fascinating insight into Friel's own process as a playwright.

But fascinating as it is structurally, in production the play seems to lose itself in its own cleverness, as if Friel is fighting a losing battle with the unruly set of characters with whom, through the character of Sir he has begun to share power. When Anna tries to pre-empt the play's climactic moment by revealing her love affair with Ben an Act too early, Sir holds her in check, but the damage to the therapeutic process, which the play pretends to set up, is done. Like the other plays we have looked at, the tension between private truth and public perception is still at issue, with the whole family complicit in preserving the image they have of themselves. ("It doesn't matter if it's true or not. It's part of the Butler lore.") But these delusions lose their potency when placed within the theatrical superstructure of Sir's overwhelming control.

Living Quarters can be seen as an important staging-post in the development of Friel's craft as a dramatist. It seems to put to the test many of the ideas that have begun to coalesce throughout his previous work. The Brechtian experiments in 'Winners' and *The Freedom of the City* come together with the idea of character as intercessor that can be seen in *The Loves of Cass Maguire* to create in Sir the ultimate mediator between the action and the audience. It is a priestly role; a spiritual role. And it sets the stage for one of Friel's greatest achievements, the play where his dextrous manipulation of various versions of the truth empowers the audience by revealing themselves in an almost Calvinistic way. That play is *Faith Healer* (1979).

With *Faith Healer*, Brian Friel reinvented the idea of drama by returning to its roots in storytelling. The audience must be attentive in order to decode its hidden truths, because the play distils the evidence which in other plays is dispersed among a wide range of characters into the testimonies of just three witnesses, who each engage directly with the audience. In this way Friel combines the full emotional and empathetic experience of naturalistic drama with the forensic clarity of epic theatre. We do not need to know if the world we see is literally real. The few fixed reference points, like the permanent presence of the poster advertising "The Fantastic Francis Hardy, Faith Healer, One Night Only" may upset the logic of what we see, but the play asserts its own theatrical logic in an extraordinarily bewitching way. The play has a subtlety that demands an exceptional delicacy in performance beyond all but the most accomplished actors.

We first meet Frank, who unfolds for us an account of his life, his faith, his friendships. Then Grace (is she Frank's mistress or his wife?). Then Teddy. Then Frank again. And much as Friel in his 'Self-Portrait' described "a dissonance, an unease" with his memory of his day's fishing with his father, we begin to realise that everything is not as it seems. Was Frank in Scotland when he heard about his mother's death, or as Grace reports, were they in Wales? Was it Frank's idea to return to Ireland or Teddy's? And by the simple but devastating means of having just a few key facts recur verbatim in each account we come to realise the awful significance of that night in Ballybeg which is to be Frank's last. Is it recklessness, vanity or despair that causes him to go that one step too far with "the savage bloody men" whose wheelchair-bound friend he seeks to heal? And yet his murderers are all too familiar. These are the same 'Boys' whom Gar drinks with and despises in *Philadelphia, Here I Come!* As the critic, Richard Pine, observes, Frank Hardy is Private Gar come home to Ballybeg.

This chapter has sought to trace the course of Brian Friel's experimentation with form from the first stirrings of a rampant theatricality in *Philadelphia, Here I Come!*, through the laboratories of *The Loves of Cass Maguire*, *Lovers*, *Living Quarters*. At every stage, Friel seeks to extend his ideas in a different direction, until finally, with *Faith Healer*, like Frank Hardy himself, he allows himself a leap of faith. In place of the more self-conscious theatricality of the earlier plays, he finds a seamless engagement with the audience's attention in the deft unfolding of his tale.

3

Heritage

1979 was a cardinal year in the course of Friel's writing. The premiere of *Faith Healer* in New York in April followed closely on the heels of his latest Abbey premiere, *Aristocrats* in March. And in May, as his 'Sporadic Diary', reveals, work began in earnest on his acknowledged masterpiece, *Translations*. In a little more than a year, not only would he have completed the new play; he would also have founded with the actor Stephen Rea (who was playing Eamon in *Aristocrats*) the Field Day Theatre Company, which for the next eight years would become the principle vehicle for his work.

We have seen in the previous chapter, how through a succession of experiments Friel refined his technique of revealing through his drama the complexities of private truth. In *Aristocrats,* with its evident Chekhovian resonances, he begins to cast his net wider to encompass a broader sense of the human condition, and in particular a sense of national identity. His diary entry for 31st August 1976 records the first stirrings of the play as:

> a family saga of three generations; articulate people, wondering about themselves and ferreting into concepts of Irishness ...
> Would it be a method of writing to induce a flatness, a quiet, an emptiness, and then to work like a farm labourer out of that dull passivity?

The image of the farm labourer reminds us of the heavy demands of the dramatist's craft. Not for nothing do we use the word 'playwright' with its sense of painstaking craftsmanship – a reality all too evident in Friel's 'Sporadic Diaries'.

Like *Faith Healer*, *Aristocrats* is about a homecoming, but whereas Frank Hardy's story is constantly guiding us towards its climax, *Aristocrats*, as Friel's diary suggests, works more by evoking an atmosphere. This is a timeless world, not only in that it seems unchanging, but also in the way in which it is no respecter of chronology. We are introduced to Ballybeg Hall in the company of Tom Hoffnung, the American academic who is seeking to capture the house's fragile history before it disintegrates completely. Elsewhere, Friel has written of the risk of a play "shout(ing) what ought to be overheard". No such a charge could be levelled against *Aristocrats*. It is an essay in eavesdropping, exemplified by the use of a baby alarm in the first scene. This relays to the listening Tom an intimate scene between the invalid Mr Justice O'Donnell, the paterfamilias who dominates the world of the play at a distance, and his long-suffering daughter Judith, whom he verbally abuses in his delusional senility, even as she tends to his every need.

Tom eagerly records unlikely episodes of family history, each one triggered by a household object named for a famous visitor, until his informant, the household's wayward son Casimir (Friel's own middle name!), finally gives himself away by claiming to have met the poet Yeats who had died two months before Casimir was born. We are, it seems, back to Friel's fascination with the idea of a constructed history. But *Aristocrats* takes this idea further into what amounts to an entire family mythology. As Casimir's usually cynical brother-in-law, Eamon, observes: "There are ... certain truths ... which are beyond Tom's kind of scrutiny". These truths are (as Hugh will later say in *Translations*) "immemorially posited" and independent of the strictures of conventional memory.

Although we see this world in decline (its power spent, the older characters who wielded it either silent or raving, its inheritors damaged and impotent), it still retains an extraordinary resilience. The whole house has acquired, in Eamon's phrase, "a permanent pigmentation" of tradition. Our brief experience of Ballybeg Hall seems suspended in time so that even as the play ends, Friel tells us that "one has the impression that this afternoon – easy, relaxed, relaxing – may go on indefinitely". Contrast and compare the picture we see of Commandant Frank Butler's house in *Living Quarters*. There, the characters seemed destined perpetually to relive the pivotal moment of their story in a kind of 'Groundhog Day'. In *Aristocrats*, there is no real story to relive – only a mood, an atmosphere, a culture to savour.

Even as *Aristocrats* was in production at the Abbey, Friel's new project, the play that was to become *Translations*, must have been taking shape in his mind. His 'Sporadic Diary' for 1979 records his progress. In mid-May he reports "returning to the same texts: the letters of John O'Donovan, Colby's *Memoir, A Paper Landscape* by John Andrews, *The Hedge Schools of Ireland* by (P.J.) Dowling, Steiner's *After Babel* ... For some reason the material resists the fusion of its disparate parts into one whole." Friel has traced the roots of the play to two "accidental discoveries": that his great-great-grandfather had been a hedge-school master and that the first trigono-metrical base for the Ordnance Survey was set up in 1828 just across the River Foyle from where he now lives. Colonel Colby was the man in charge of the survey. John O'Donovan (like Owen in *Translations*) was his orthographer, responsible for verifying the correct spellings of place names. In John Andrews' book, *A Paper Landscape*, he found "the perfect metaphor to accommodate and realize all those shadowy notions – map-making". But the real catalyst in Friel's creative process was George Steiner's *After Babel,* some of which was to find its way directly into the final play.

Friel had come across *After Babel* when he was working on his adaptation of Chekhov's *Three Sisters*. Working between half a dozen existing translations, he became intrigued by the multiplicity of nuances that distinguished the different English versions of the same play. Steiner's work provided a theoretical explanation for the process of translation:

> Any model of communication is at the same time a model of translation ... No two historical epochs, no two social classes, no two localities, use words and syntax to signify exactly the same things ... All communication interprets between privacies.

Not only does this particularity of language justify the need for a constant renewal of the extant translations of foreign language texts, such as Friel's *Three Sisters* with its distinctive Irish vocabulary and cadences; it also became the spiritual centre of the play, *Translations*.

On 14th May 1979, Friel recorded in his diary the play's crucial question:

> The people of Ballybeg would have been Irish-speaking in
> 1833. So a theatrical conceit will have to be devised by which
> – even though the actors speak English – the audience will
> assume or accept that they are speaking Irish. Could that work?

The subsequent production history of the play confirms that the answer is a resounding 'yes!'. What makes it work is the capacity of subtle variations in both the written and spoken use of English, combined with the given circumstances of each scene, to allow an audience to understand seamlessly whether the language they are hearing is English-as-English or English-as-Irish. The importance of the oral component of this process was clarified by an American production of *Translations* in which Owen spoke with an English accent when speaking English and an Irish accent when speaking Irish. Friel implicitly acknowledged this point when he came to write his 1986 play, *Making History*, and indicated in the stage directions that its central character should have two distinct accents – a public and a private presence in the one voice.

Friel's antipathy towards the direct engagement by dramatists in politics is well documented and he has commented that "Ireland does not seem to infuse her writers with ... political zeal. Or to put it another way: Irishmen and women with that kind of vision and commitment find modes other than the arts through which to express themselves." Undoubtedly, still mindful of the one-dimensional reception of *The Freedom of the City*, his diary reveals an early anxiety about the true nature of his latest play:

> The thought occurred to me that what I was circling around
> was a political play and that thought panicked me. But it is a
> political play – how can that be avoided? If it is not political,
> what is it? Inaccurate history? Social drama?

But by 1st June his aim is clear:

> The play has to do with language and only language. And if it
> becomes overwhelmed by (the) political element, it is lost.

Despite the assertion of Friel's old friend and Field Day Board Member, Seamus Heaney, that the company liked to think it had "less a position than a disposition", the Opening Night of *Translations* on 23rd September 1980 in Derry's Guildhall could not fail to have had political significance. This had, after all, been the setting for *The Freedom of the City*. Key figures on both sides of Northern Ireland's normally rigidly observed political divide joined in the unanimous applause. Field Day's manifesto may have invoked a 'fifth province' of the imagination, but the divided state of Ulster, one of Ireland's four historic provinces, was still very much at the heart of contemporary sensibilities. Nevertheless, the immediate experience of coming to the play without the expectations that its subsequent familiarity has engendered must have disarmed even the most unsympathetic members of the audience. The 19th-century setting created immediate distance. The rich variety of characters (not least Liam Neeson's energetic Doalty) and the eccentricity of the hedge school with its adult learners and grandiloquent schoolmaster must surely have engaged all who saw them. While some London critics took exception to the representation of the English army officers as being ignorant of Latin, in the full flow of performance it is easy to see how the soldiers lack of comprehension could be explained by the fact this Latin was being spoken by the extravagantly rustic Jimmy Jack, presumably with a heavy accent. (Even some Dubliners reported difficulty understanding all of the Northern 'brogue').

The hilarity of the desperate attempts by Captain Lancey, the army cartographer, to make his English understood to the Irish speaking peasantry would surely have struck a chord with anyone who had had a foreign holiday, and the 'bi-lingual' love scene in which the audience is privy to the exchanged intimacies of both Maire (the Irish colleen) and Lieutenant Yolland (the chocolate box soldier incarnate) while the lovers themselves struggle for meaning, must have been as enchanting as it was unexpected. Even the densely scripted map-making scene in which Hugh's son Owen, newly returned from Dublin and in the army's employ, begins to question his faith in a new English-speaking order in the face of Yolland's passion for the bewitching Irish names, cannot have been less than fascinating. In the wake of such theatrical delights, the violence of the final act, with Yolland's presumed death and Lancey's brutal retribution must have been shocking, but also so sudden as to defy immediate analysis.

In short, it is my belief that the play in its first performance lived up to Friel's hopes for it as he had earlier expressed them in his diary. On 22nd June 1979 he had contrasted the idea of the "actual thing" (the circumstantial content) with the "ideal thing" – "the inner core". On the 6th July he added:

> One of the mistakes of the direction in which the play is presently pulling is the almost wholly *public* concern of the theme: how does the eradication of the Irish language and the substitution of English affect this particular *society*? ... The play must concern itself only with the exploration of the dark and private places of individual souls.

This aim was achievable on stage, but once the text was published and isolated from the immediate experience of seeing it performed, the essential humanity of Friel's drama rapidly risked becoming overwhelmed by the weight of detailed historical criticism. The historian Sean Connolly took exception to the portrayal of the British army Ordnance Survey unit as a brutally repressive force terrorising the Donegal countryside with fixed bayonets, and viewed the play as "a crude portrayal of cultural and military imperialism visited on passive victims". But Connolly's error was in seeking to objectify the subjective. While the weight of historical evidence may well justify such indignation, the play, as Friel argues clearly in the above diary entry, is conceived not as a universal historical truth, but as a particular reality. The account we hear of from Bridget and Doalty of the British military response, for all its undoubted hysteria, is essentially a comic one, and speaks of only fifty soldiers. Even Lancey's ultimatum smacks more of bluster than ruthless retribution. This is, after all, the slightly ridiculous character whom Yolland characterises as "the perfect colonial servant", a stickler for proper procedure.

Similarly, when literary critics such as Edna Longley accused Friel of reinforcing rather than examining "myths of dispossession and oppression", they made too little allowance for the ambivalence with which Friel had conjured up a romanticised image of a glorious Gaelic past to which he states in his diary he cannot give credence. Hugh at his most grandiloquent is described as "deliberately parodying himself". As Seamus Heaney has put it, *Translations* is as much "irony" as "elegy". Much of the criticism says more about the subjectivity of the critics than about Friel's. What it does show clearly is the huge difficulty of reading the printed text as if it were the dramatic event itself, and the risk entailed even in treating one performance as a definitive reading of a play. As we have already pointed out, no two productions are the same, nor any two performances even of the same production.

The most perceptive analysis was that offered by another historian, J.H. Andrews, whose book about the Ordnance Survey was one of Friel's key sources. He found the play "an extremely subtle blend of historical truth – and some other kind of truth". He viewed the play:

> as a set of images that might have been painted on screens, each depicting some passage of Irish history, ancient or modern, the screens placed one behind the other in a tunnel with a light at one end of the tunnel and the audience at the other, so that it is only the strongest colours and the boldest lines that appear in the composite picture exhibited on the stage. On this reading Captain Lancey's brutal threats would be justified as projections … from some quite different period of history.

This powerful theatrical metaphor recalls Friel's own thoughts when embarking on the writing of *Aristocrats*:

> 17th September 1976 – A dozen false starts. And the problem with false starts is that once they are attempted, written down, they tend to become actual, blood-related to the whole. So that finally each false start will have to be dealt with, adjusted, absorbed. Like life.

He might equally have been talking about Irish history! Andrews' complex analogy can just as readily be related to the layers of archaeological history in *Volunteers* and the apparent timelessness of *Aristocrats* itself. It also recalls the echoes in *Translations* of various emblems of Irish theatre history – Synge's Hiberno-English cadences, the Wildean symmetry of the love scene at the end of the first part of Act Two, and the final scene where Hugh and Jimmy Jack become latterday shadows of O'Casey's Joxer and Captain Boyle from *Juno and the Paycock*. It is because Friel is often erroneously thought of as a naturalistic writer that he becomes vulnerable to the sort of criticism levelled against *Translations*. No-one would think of making the same critique of Stewart Parker's *Northern Star* (1984), which is applauded for its more self-conscious use of the stylistic palette of Anglo-Irish drama.

It is arguably the legacy of the mainly naturalistic theatre of the early 20th century that makes this issue worthy of comment at all. Of its very nature, historical drama juxtaposes the present and the past in the very proximity of the audience to the action. Shakespeare's audience does not seem to have been troubled by the presence of the new technology of striking clocks in Julius Caesar's Rome. It seems perverse, then, to be troubled by the prominence of Virgil and Homer amidst the potatoes and turf of 19th-century Ballybeg. Perhaps for this reason, when discussing a design concept for my own production of *Translations* I found myself using Shelley's sonnet, *Ozymandias,* as a reference point. Written in 1818 at the height of the Romantic period, it evokes the pervasive sense of change that followed the French Revolution and that had so inspired Yolland's own father:

> I met a traveller from an antique land
> Who said: Two vast and trunkless legs of stone
> Stand in the desert. Near them, on the sand,
> Half sunk, a shattered visage lies, whose frown,
> And wrinkled lip, and sneer of cold command,
> Tell that its sculptor well those passions read
> Which yet survive, stamped on these lifeless things,
> The hand that mocked them and the heart that fed;
> And on the pedestal these words appear:
> "My name is Ozymandias, king of kings:
> Look on my works, ye Mighty, and despair!"
> Nothing beside remains. Round the decay
> Of that colossal wreck, boundless and bare
> The lone and level sands stretch far away.

Hugh aspires to the same sense of the eternal. Like Ozymandias his world is about to be swept away. Unlike Shelley's ancient potentate, however, he seems prepared to abandon the romance of history and bend to the wind. His agreement to teach English and his determination to "make these new names (his) own" makes him an unlikely symbol of a bogus romantic nationalism. This is a man who despite his age is prepared for change. His dilemma is reminiscent of the characters that have drawn Friel to late 19th century Russian drama, who in Friel's own words, "behave as if their old certainties were as sustaining as ever – even though they know in their hearts that their society is in meltdown and the future has neither a welcome nor an accommodation for them". But it is Owen, the younger man, not Hugh, who seems determined to champion the old ways. It is the play's great achievement that it can seamlessly accommodate both ideas. But as with *The Freedom of the City*, critics and audiences have been too quick to understand the perspective of one or other character as Friel's own.

Understandably, if unfairly, the welter of criticism about the perceived inaccuracy of *Translations* seems to have affected Friel to an extent that casts doubt on his claimed indifference to the critics. Unusually, he engaged in a direct response to J.H. Andrews' criticism in the periodical journal *The Crane Bag*, declaring that "drama is first a fiction, with the authority of fiction. You do not go to *Macbeth* for history". And his next three plays for Field Day all in their different ways seem to be a continuation of the argument by other means. Friel's adaptation of Chekhov's *Three Sisters* was Field Day's choice for their second tour that followed *Translations* in 1981. Friel had begun working on it before he wrote *Translations*, and it reflects many of the same preoccupations, particularly in relation to the importance of acknowledging the unique nature of the English spoken in Ireland. That Hugh's wit and erudition is communicated to us through the medium of English is ironic insofar as it signifies the ultimate eclipse of the Gaelic culture he holds so dear. But at the same time, what the critic Nicholas Grene describes as "his fluent and capacious" use of English is eloquent testimony to the way in which the Irish have made the usurper language their own.

This was the spirit that Friel breathed into Chekhov. As he told Ciaran Carty in Dublin's *Sunday Independent* in the run-up to *Translations*: "The assumption ... is that we speak the same language as England. We don't". And again, in an interview (with Paddy Agnew): "This is something about which I feel strongly – in some way we are constantly overshadowed by the sound of the English language, as well as the printed word ... Twenty miles from where we are sitting, you can hear very strong elements of Elizabethan English being spoken every day ... We must make English identifiably our own language". *Three Sisters* was more, therefore, than a homage to the great Russian dramatist he so admired. (The director, Conall Morrison has said that Friel's whole life has been a dialogue with Chekhov.) It was as much an assertion of Ireland's claim to be at the heart of European culture as Hugh's assimilation of the *Iliad* and the *Aeneid*.

The power of Chekhov to make his presence felt across the whole continent of Europe, and of the influence of Homer and Virgil to span millennia, are examples of what I like to think of as 'cultural gravity'. The laws of cultural gravity are similar to Newton's own. The attraction exerted by a city, for instance, is dependent both on its cultural mass and its distance from its subject. It is an inclusive concept, acknowledging the fact that interdependent influences can co-exist with one another. Applied to the specific issue of language and translation, this idea can help explain the tenacity of local usage in the face of seemingly overwhelming external pressures – hence Friel's example of the survival of Elizabethan English in Donegal. The critic, Elmer Andrews, relates this process to the ideas of the Russian theorist, Mikhail Bakhtin, who identified a "dynamic tension" between "centrifugal" and "centripetal" influences at work in the evolution of language. The pressure to conform to a centralised norm (such as the seemingly pervasive spread in the South East of England of 'Estuary English'), is counter-balanced by the consciously subversive attraction of local vocabularies and turns of phrase. It is one way in which communities can assert their diversity within the increasing universality of English as a lingua franca.

Given that it predated it, the relevance of Friel's version of *Three Sisters* to the increasing controversy that was growing around *Translations* was largely coincidental. For Field Day's 1982 tour, Friel responded directly to the debate with a deliberately subversive counterpart to his earlier play. *The Communication Cord* is set in the present, but when Jack shows his friend Tim around his father's lovingly restored facsimile of a 19th-century Donegal cottage, he might just as easily be the stage manager of *Translations* describing the details of the set for the earlier play. The form is broad farce which Friel had last attempted with his political satire, *The Mundy Scheme,* in 1969. The poor reception that that play had received cannot have provided Friel with much encouragement, but the first act of the new play positively crackles with wit. Tim is a junior lecturer in linguistics, allowing ample scope for poking fun at some of the preoccupations of *Translations.* The influence of Steiner becomes even more explicit, with much exposition of the idea of encoded messages which language can conceal. Friel's earlier fascination with individual truth finds farcical form in multiple mistaken identities. And the play is replete with in-jokes, as when the eminent Senator Doctor Donovan finds himself imitating a calf, much as Yolland has done in his attempts to woo Maire. And when the lights go out at the midpoint climax, there are clear echoes of the linguistic chaos of the Tower of Babel.

The play loses energy and direction in the second half, and Friel may have come to regret the self-indulgence of committing the fortunes of Field Day so resolutely to this kind of riposte, but his point could not be clearer. The play is a denial of an overt romanticism about Ireland's Gaelic past, and recalls Gerald McNamara's 1907 Abbey Theatre satire on Synge, *The Mist that Do be on the Bog,* in which northern cultural explorers seek out the 'true wesht' in Connemara inspired by *The Playboy of the Western World,* only to discover that the rustic peasant they find there is actually an amateur playwright from suburban Dublin.

The Communication Cord proved to be the last of the "Friels on Wheels" for more than half a decade as Field Day turned to other writers in subsequent years, but in 1988 came Friel's considered response to the continuing controversy around *Translations.* Even the title, *Making History,* seemed to advertise his intentions. In a programme note for the production he made these crystal clear:

> *Making History* is a dramatic fiction that uses some actual and some imagined events in the life of Hugh O'Neill to make a story. I have tried to be objective, faithful – after my artistic fashion – to the empirical method. But when there was a tension between historical 'fact' and the imperative of the fiction, I'm glad to say I have kept faith with the narrative … Part of me regrets taking occasional liberties. But then I remind myself that history and fiction are related and comparable forms of

discourse and that an historical text is a kind of literary artefact.

To reinforce his point he introduces the character of Archbishop Peter Lombard who is engaged in chronicling the life of the play's hero, Hugh O'Neill. The enterprise clearly fills its subject with some unease:

O'Neill   And I hear you're writing our history, Peter …

Lombard   I'll just try and tell the story of what I saw and took part in as accurately as I can.

O'Neill   But you'll tell the truth? …

Lombard   If you're asking me will my story be as accurate as possible – of course it will. But are truth and falsity the proper criteria? I don't know. Maybe when the time comes my first responsibility will be to tell the best possible narrative. Isn't that what history is, a kind of story-telling?

O'Neill   But where does the truth come into all of this?

Lombard   I'm not sure that 'truth' is a primary ingredient – is that a shocking thing to say? Maybe when the time comes, imagination will be as important as information.

If the controversy over *Translations* had deflected the trajectory of Friel's creative journey, here he seems to be making a new covenant with himself. His wilderness years were over. He would forsake the tyrannous expectations of history and return home. Fearless like Frank Hardy, he would pursue his destiny to reveal the intimate but universal truths of Ballybeg.

4

Home

The opening night of *Dancing at Lughnasa* at the Abbey Theatre in 1990 will live long in my memory. The visual impact of Joe Vanek's set with its cutaway cottage nestling beneath a towering swathe of ripe corn made an immediate impression and as the action unfolded the depth of characterisation of each of the five sisters left an indelible legacy in my mind. At the end of the play, the response from the audience was immediate and euphoric, and although I recall a certain irritation at what I felt at the time was an excessive use of narration – a tendency to tell where we could have been shown – I shared the general enthusiasm. Returning to the printed text more than a decade later, I have a clearer sense of precisely how the play works, and more patience with the use of the narrative frame.

Comparisons between *Dancing at Lughnasa* and Tennessee Williams' *The Glass Menagerie* (which Judy Friel directed in the Abbey's studio theatre, the Peacock, to coincide with the opening of her father's own play) are inevitable. Each presents its story through the medium of a narrator who has been part of the action, and who is grateful to have escaped the claustrophobic restrictions of the domestic world each play describes. To that extent, *Dancing at Lughnasa* can fairly be categorised as a 'memory play'. But as we have seen in the preceding chapters, Friel has made the representation of memory on stage his life's work, and it is not enough simply to equate this play with another more than fifty years its senior. The reality we see in *Lughnasa* obeys its own unique theatrical logic evident in embryo in earlier plays such as *Living Quarters* and 'Winners'. As Friel has his narrator, Michael, explain, "in that memory, atmosphere is more real than incident and everything is simultaneously actual and illusory".

As with the film imagery discussed above in relation to *Philadelphia, Here I Come!*, memory in *Dancing at Lughnasa* seems to flow from a still image represented in tableau at the start of the play and returned to at its end. Uncle Jack, the wayward missionary who has just returned from Uganda to Ballybeg hints at this key device when he recalls his own memory of leaving Ballybeg as a "camera-picture" or a photograph. In this way, for all its use of narration as a framing device, the play is anything but a narrative. And in a supposedly logocentric Irish theatre culture, *Lughnasa* stands out for the way in which the language of movement becomes a central motif. As Michael concludes, his memories are dominated not by words but by music and dancing:

> as if language had surrendered to movement – as if this ritual, this wordless ceremony, was now the way to speak, to whisper private and sacred things, to be in touch with some otherness … Dancing as if language no longer existed because words were no longer necessary.

While this denial of words is certainly startling in the context of Irish drama, it is entirely consistent with Friel's developing stagecraft. The reference to the whispering of "private and sacred things" recalls the notion of "privacies" in *Translations* and the importance of the idea of ritual in Friel's work goes back at least as far as his time with Tyrone Guthrie in Minneapolis who viewed theatre "as the direct descendant of primitive religious ceremonies". This relationship was given detailed expression by the anthropologist Victor Turner, who identified the idea of "liminality" as its defining feature. That is to say, theatre and ritual both operate on a threshold allowing the possibility of transition from one state to another. In the case of *Dancing at Lughnasa* the threshold is between a traditional rural order and a modern industrial one. Michael's father, Gerry Evans is lured, however disingenuous he may seem, by the progressive ideology of the International Brigade while Uncle Jack evokes vivid images of native Ryangan rituals similar to those that form the basis of Turner's work.

For Michael's upright (and uptight!) Aunt Kate these seemingly opposite forces of primitive paganism and "godless communism" both represent a threat to her status quo. And yet the residual primitivism of rural Ireland is evident in reports of harvest rituals only fields away. The character of Uncle Jack recalls many of the themes of *Translations*. His struggle to recall English words reminds us of how crucial language is to identity, just as it was for the mute Sarah in the earlier play. And his revelation that he has spurned English investment in favour of the maintenance of the traditional Ryangan way of life contrasts with the readiness of the Irish to adopt English culture that seems to be the triumphant trend in *Translations*.

In his diary entry for 18th June 1979 as he was writing *Translations* Friel noted:

> In Ballybeg, at the point when the play begins, the cultural climate is a dying climate – no longer quickened by its past, about to be plunged into an alien future. The victims in this situation are the transitional generation. The old can retreat into and find immunity in the past. The young acquire some facility with the new cultural implements. The in-between ages become lost, wandering around in a strange land. Strays.

In *Dancing at Lughnasa*, the Mundy sisters find themselves in this middle-ground.

A central metaphor for this transition is Marconi, the radio set, which uses the latest technology to introduce the primitive strains of the traditional music that triggers the play's most famous scene – the moment when the sisters dance. The rapid development of a distinctly 'physical theatre' in Ireland has been one of the defining features of Irish drama in the 1990s. But *Lughnasa* differs from such productions as Marie Jones' highly physical *Stones in his Pockets* or the Barrabas Theatre Company's strikingly physical reinvention of Lennox Robinson's classic well-made play *The White Headed Boy*. In Friel's play, the physicality is integral to the text rather than developed by actors and a director in rehearsal. His meticulous description of the dance repays close attention. In particular, the precise manner in which each sister engages with the action, and crucially the order in which they both enter and exit from the spectacle is clearly delineated.

A crucial note is that "there is a sense of order being consciously subverted". The term suggests a connection with the ideas of the Russian theorist, Mikhail Bakhtin, and his analysis of the "carnivalesque". Just as the medieval Feast of Fools, in which once a year the Lord of Misrule presided over a festival in which kings humbled themselves before clowns, provided an essential safety valve for a society rigorously regulated by a strict religious orthodoxy, so in Bakhtin's view apparently sophisticated modern societies also need their outlets. In *Lughnasa*, Rose fulfils the role of the clown or 'fool' able to say what others can't, revealing suppressed truths. Dance satisfies their essential need for the carnivalesque.

For while there may be superficial comparisons with the sexual repressiveness of Lorca's *House of Bernarda Alba*, with its cast of women starved of male company, Kate is no Bernarda Alba, as the frequent glimpses Friel allows us of her underlying weakness makes clear. It is above all in their dancing that each of the characters reveal themselves to us. It may seem strange that so powerful a theatrical device occurs so early in the play, rather than providing a crowning climax. But the effectiveness of its timing in performance is to provide a context for all that follows. Its energy creates a wave that rolls on to the end of the first act, across the interval and throughout the rest of the play.

Apart from the use of ritual movement, the other most striking characteristic of *Dancing at Lughnasa* is the way in which Friel continues his experiments with the metatheatrical – the way in which the play expressly acknowledges its own artificiality. The invisibility for the audience of the young Michael while the rest of the cast appear able to see him is paralleled in Maggie's evocation of an invisible bird, the unreality of which she uses to tease her young nephew. Friel seems almost to be toying with the audience's sense of themselves as detached observers.

Michael's own role as narrator is complicated by his apparent inclusion in scenes as his younger self but with his present voice. The device of allowing the narrator to foreshadow the future is here used much more tellingly than in 'Winners' because it is organically connected to the telling of the story rather than seeking to achieve a Brechtian neutrality. Whereas actors playing the narrators in the earlier play often report profound difficulty in achieving the detachment indicated by Friel, in *Lughnasa*, the additional knowledge provided for the audience by Michael, who is emotionally connected to the events on stage, unquestionably raises the emotional stakes of the subsequent scenes. Friel most displays his craftsmanship in the deft way in which he reveals essential information, as in the oblique and indirect manner in which the thwarting of Kate's matrimonial ambitions is revealed. Because the news reaches the audience's ears on Maggie's lips, the effect is even more poignant than when Madge in *Philadelphia, Here I Come!* makes her seemingly casual reference that the new baby will be called not Madge but Agnes.

The enormous international success of *Dancing at Lughnasa* consolidated Friel's status as Ireland's most important living playwright and ensured that his work would be in constant demand by Dublin's leading managements for the next decade. Plans were immediately set in train for his next Abbey production, *Wonderful Tennessee*, and most unusually for an unknown play, his producer, Noel Pearson, was able to count on strong Broadway interest from the outset. The phenomenal international success of *Dancing at Lughnasa* must also have brought Friel complete financial security. Perhaps for this reason, his plays since *Lughnasa* have reflected a more introspective journey of personal reflection. Friel has written about the underlying motivation for each play in terms of necessity, echoing Ibsen's idea of "the necessary lie". Thus *Dancing at Lughnasa* demonstrates "the necessity for paganism", *Wonderful Tennessee* explores "the necessary mystery", *Molly Sweeney*, "the necessary vigilance" and *Give Me Your Answer, Do!* "the necessary uncertainty". It seems almost as if having struggled for inspiration through the 1980s, the plays of the 1990s carry their own inner driving force.

Mystery in *Wonderful Tennessee* is symbolised by Oileán Draíochta, the Island of Otherness out of reach in the mist across the sea. Three couples in their late thirties and early forties arrive at a pier after a four-hour drive from the conventional civilisation of (presumably) Dublin. With varying degrees of patience, they wait for nearly two days for Mr Carlin, the boatman to take them across to the island. And while they wait they talk and sing, freely mixing the sublime with the profane. Most of the play proceeds at a rattling pace punctuated by only a few more reflective sections in which the history of the island is explained.

It begins in legend, with the island appearing only once every seven years before disappearing back into the mist. Then visitors like those in Friel's earlier play, *The Gentle Island*, perhaps, or like

Prometheus in Greek myth, light a fire destroying its magic. We hear also of the medieval monks who lived on the island and saw visions and the local youths who were involved in some rumoured sacrificial rite in 1932. But unlike the Mundy sisters, these modern city dwellers are far removed from their primitive past and are quick to explain away the mysterious. But they can also acknowledge that, as *Translations* shows, "language stands baffled" in the face of mystery and has "no vocabulary for the experience". Perhaps for this reason, words seem debased in *Wonderful Tennessee*. This is not a poetic play, but it is rich in banal ritual. Like Beckett's tramps in *Waiting for Godot*, the characters wait for a deliverance that never comes – in this case represented by Mr Carlin, a latter day counterpart to Charon who in Greek mythology ferried the dead across the River Styx. And again unlike the Mundy sisters who are still capable of being touched by ancient lore, these more familiar characters ultimately fail to embrace the otherness they come to find. They are the disinherited descendants of the families that abandon *The Gentle Island*. As Friel had described Cass Maguire's family to Hilton Edwards, they are:

> the *new Irish*, the Harrys who have made money and drive big cars and golf at the Hermitage, and who have forgotten that their fathers were tatty-hokers in Scotland.

The "necessary vigilance" refers to the failure of the eye-surgeon in *Molly Sweeney* to understand the full impact of his craft. Of all Friel's plays, *Molly Sweeney* is closest in form to *Faith Healer* in that it consists of a series of monologues delivered by two males and one female. But as the title suggests, the focal character in this case is the woman. Molly Sweeney has been blind from early childhood, but her husband Frank has convinced himself that she can be made to see. Mr Rice is the eye surgeon, who like Frank Hardy in *Faith Healer*, has lost confidence in his own powers. The story unfolds from their various perspectives, and Molly Sweeney has her sight partially restored. But it brings with it a sort of madness. In losing her blindness she loses her own sense of herself. In this regard, the play links back to Friel's earlier explorations of the intimate complexity of individual identity. The play is also a contemporary reworking of Synge's *The Well of the Saints* in which two blind beggars lose the illusion of their own beauty when their sight is restored and end up choosing to return to their blind state. But Friel uses the characters of Rice and Frank to interpolate extensive references to a scientific and philosophical understanding of Molly Sweeney's plight, much as Hugh becomes the conduit for Steiner's musings on the nature of language.

The play also casts new light on the relationship between the artist's life and work. The section of his published diary that relates to the writing of *Molly Sweeney* makes it clear that he was himself understandably preoccupied with problems with his own sight which seems to have driven his interest in the subject. The extent to which knowledge of such a fact informs our understanding of the play is one to which we will return in our discussion of *Performances* in the final chapter.

Finally, we come to "the necessary uncertainty". If *Philadelphia, Here I Come!* can be said to be Friel's *Hamlet*, 'Winners' his *Romeo & Juliet*, *Living Quarters* his *Othello*, *Translations* his *Tempest*, and *Making History* his *Macbeth*. *Give Me Your Answer, Do!* is his *King Lear*. Just as Shakespeare through Lear reflects on the perspective of an older man reviewing his life's work, so Tom Connolly, the protagonist of Friel's most recent full-length play, presents us with a writer seeking to come to terms with his relationship to posterity. The play opens with Tom visiting his daughter in a mental asylum. She seems wholly unable to communicate but he talks to her at length, setting the scene for the ensuing play. Some critics have likened her to his frustrated muse, for Tom, like Friel in so many of his most poignant diary entries, is suffering from writer's block. The various house guests (his wife's parents, another writer and his wife and an agent from an American university eager to buy up his personal archive) inhabit a similar kind of neo-Chekhovian world to the one evoked in *Aristocrats*. This is not a comfortable world, but it is a strikingly honest one. It is, in the end, the situation's greatest victim, his wife Daisy, who finally explains his need not to accept the easy reassurance and financial reward of the academic respectability that selling his papers would provide:

> Because that uncertainty is necessary. He must live with that uncertainty, that necessary uncertainty. Because there can be no verdicts, no answers. Indeed there must be no verdicts.

Because being alive is the postponement of verdicts, isn't it? Because verdicts are provided only when it's all over, all concluded.

In 1972, Friel hoped in his 'Self-Portrait' that between then and his death he would "have required a religion, a philosophy, a sense of life that will make it less frightening than it appears ... at this moment." By 1997 his thinking has moved on. Unlike Frank Hardy in *Faith Healer*, in *Give Me Your Answer, Do!* Brian Friel seems at last to be becoming more at ease with chance. The Irish word *baile*, which appears in Baile Beag, though usually translated as 'town' can also carry the meaning 'home'. And it is this sense that most applies to Friel's later plays. Cass Maguire, Gabriel in *Crystal and Fox*, Ben in *Living Quarters*, Casimir in *Aristocrats* and Owen in *Translations* all fail to make a satisfactory homecoming. Since *Lughnasa*, however, Friel has allowed himself a certain introspection. Freed of his preoccupations with sweeping themes of history and heritage he has brought his drama closer home.

5

Exploring Ballybeg

Having set the scene, it is now time to begin our exploration of Ballybeg. The following accounts of productions are not offered as in any way definitive. Rather they are intended to illustrate the subjective nature of play production, and that no matter how far a director's priority is to realise faithfully the author's intention, the whole process is so governed by specific elements, that it is inevitable that a distinctive response to the text will emerge from each new production. I would further suggest that this is not just inevitable, but necessary to ensure the vitality of the resulting piece of theatre, and I would encourage you to look afresh at each play from your own production perspective, whether this be real or imagined. You cannot effectively envision a play, without at least speculating on the possibilities of production.

Philadelphia, Here I Come!

I first saw a production of *Philadelphia, Here I Come!* at the Lyric Theatre, Belfast in 1976 with the fine Belfast actor, John Hewitt as Public Gar and Private played by a talented newcomer from the Glens of Antrim, Liam Neeson. Nearly twenty years later, in 1994, I was invited to direct the play in the same theatre, and the obvious actor to play S.B. O'Donnell was John Hewitt. Working with him on the production was a remarkable experience. I still had vivid memories of the earlier production, but for John it was as if the experience of playing Public Gar all those years ago had matured within him into an exceptionally instinctual understanding of the whole play. Every nuance, every gesture, and above all his exquisite playing of the play's silences was beautifully judged. When two years later we were invited to tour the new production in the United States, Liam Neeson, came to see the show on the last night of the tour in Hertford, Connecticut, straight from a promotional tour in Ireland of the film, *Michael Collins*. His presence undoubtedly inspired all the actors, and the performance had a heightened quality that carried over into the green room, when Neeson renewed his acquaintance with the actor whose alter-ego he had played two decades earlier.

The relationship between John Hewitt's two performances, as son and then as father, was inevitably a key element in the preparation of our production. The younger actors (Ruairi Conaghan as Public and Peter O'Meara as Private) could not help but be aware of the sense of continuity that John represented. For myself as director, it also emphasised the challenge of reviving (the technical theatre term seemed especially apt) a play that had had such a distinctive production history. One early idea, with which we experimented during the preview performances, was that we would open the play with John in 1990s clothing entering the shop set and being served by a shop assistant (played by the same actress as Kate). A musical transition provided by the Mendelssohn Violin Concerto that features so powerfully later in the play, would then cover a lighting change that would suggest a flashback into Gar's memories and the start of the play. This concept fitted with the idea of the play discussed in Chapter 2 as taking place in Gar's memory, but we decided during previews and before the official opening night that it raised unhelpful questions in the audience's mind. We retained the musical opening, but dispensed with the little 'dumb show'. Nevertheless, I believe it helped the actors place this 1990s production in relation to its 1960s origins. If Gar had emigrated to Philadelphia in 1964 (that is, the year in which the play was premiered), by 1994 he would have been approaching the age his father had been when Gar had left Ireland. It seemed to me the perfect prismatic convention through which to view the play.

The other major implication of returning to the play three decades on was the extent to which the understanding of stagecraft in Ireland had progressed in that time. The Lyric's open stage precluded the use of curtains and we decided also to minimise the number of physical entrances and exits. As indicated in Friel's stage directions, we retained the general sense of the kitchen and Gar's bedroom on separate parts of the stage, but otherwise we left the outer edges of the playing areas undefined by walls. Above and behind the playing area, Stuart Marshall, the designer, created an old-fashioned shop window with vastly oversized shop goods including massive cans of soup two metres high. This became Private Gar's playground and the location for the only scene not to take place in the O'Donnell's house – his meeting with Kate's father – thereby enhancing the sense that this flashback takes place in Gar's own mind.

The shelf was less than average human height, and at the centre of it was a traditional wooden dresser with plates and cups, with a door to one side through which all the visitors to the house entered. The fact that they had to stoop down to negotiate the corridor under the 'shelf' which connected to the stage wings created a somewhat magical impression, as if they had materialised from nowhere. Most tellingly, when Private Gar first appeared, it was up from behind the dresser, on which he sat for his first exchange with Public Gar, machine-gunning the imaginary fishing boat from this vantage point. Peter O'Meara proved to be fearlessly athletic in scrambling up and down between the stage and the 'shelf', over the table and onto Gar's wardrobe. The overall effect was to create a vivid impression of the volatility of Gar's private thoughts.

Such was the optical impact of the oversized shop window, that one school student, in a post-performance discussion, wondered how we had managed to get Private Gar to change size during the performance – a striking extension of the suspension of disbelief! By the time Gar returns to his bedroom, the entrancing double-act between Public and Private is in full swing, and continued in rehearsal to provide consistent stimulation for an inventive actor like O'Meara. When John Hewitt made his first entrance as S.B., the audience was usually fully bewitched by Private's antics, and the scene in which he predicts his father's dialogue fully capitalised on this level of engagement.

One of the most unusual structural aspects of the play is that of a cast of 14, all but five appear in only one scene. This heightens the episodic feel of the narrative. Continuity is provided mainly by Madge, the housekeeper, but also by a strong sense of S.B.'s constant unseen presence. In our production, we ran throughout the play a continuous recording of the ticking of the clock that S.B. winds in the first scene. Although this was kept at a constant volume, in performance it only became clearly audible at the moments of strongest silence. I came to think of this sound as an extension of S.B.'s personality. Following Gar's example, the audience is inclined to take Madge for granted, but to register more strongly than he does her delight at the prospect of Nelly's new baby being named after her. They also share, in a way that Gar does not, her crushing disappointment when this turns out not to be the case. As Madge in our production Maureen Dow gave a finely restrained performance, characterised in my own memory by a discussion I had with her about whether she should clear the table cloth from the table after the mealtime scene. The decision was based eventually on the subtle expressiveness of her feet which the table cloth obscured in certain scenes. It was a point not lost on Friel, who introduces her in his stage direction as walking "as if her feet were precious". Someone like Madge, who is so good at hiding her feelings, reveals herself in a sometimes surprising, non-verbal way. From Maureen's point of view, this physical stage direction provided an invaluable way into the character.

The scene ends with the visit of Gar's former schoolmaster. Frank O'Connor, the master short story writer whose work so influenced Friel, criticised the first production of *Philadelphia, Here I Come!* for turning "a beautiful, gentle play … into a rip-roaring review". But the deliberately episodic structure of the play works precisely by building the intensity of each successive scene. For this reason, Gar's encounter with Master Boyle is among the play's most delicately observed and poignant sections. Friel, a former teacher himself, and the son of a teacher, judges the vicarious sense of parenthood brilliantly.

On Boyle's embarrassed and embarrassing exit, Gar is left alone and Episode Two is more introspective. We see the visit of Gar's aunt in flashback in all the heightened awfulness with which Gar's memory imbues it. This is the first of two trios (the musical terminology is apt), with the almost silent American friend adding subtly to the tension generated by Gar's would-be adoptive parents. The second trio consists of "The boys". As we saw in Chapter 1, Hilton Edwards had proposed cutting one of the characters, but Friel held out for three. The justification of this is to be felt most in the scene's closing moment, when the youngest boy, Joe, reveals a glimpse of what Gar might become if he doesn't leave. The "sycamore trees" line is one of the play's most unexpected laugh lines. When Kate finally comes to say her farewells, Public discovers an unexpected flood of articulacy which only serves to destroy their last moment together.

The visit of the Canon in Episode Three is richly ritualistic – almost liturgical in its rigidity. Friel's genius is to fill the aching silence with Private Gar's most energetic display of inventive frustration. When our production was filmed on video as a teaching aid for schools, I was surprised on watching the tape to see that the highly visual and physical fireworks generated in this scene by Private Gar as he cavorted around, over and across the draught-playing Canon and councillor, did not feature on the tape. Instead the editor kept the camera constantly on the shadowy figure of Public Gar standing stock still in his bedroom, while the soundtrack recorded the scene next door. The effect was to bring home to me the true poignancy of the scene. In a future production, I would contrive to make the audience more aware of the listening presence of Public Gar.

The final scene in which Gar and his father struggle to connect reveals just how expressive silence can be. The non-verbal bond between them is palpable, and we can all too easily believe Madge's conclusion that when Gar is S.B.'s age he will be just the same as his father. And when Gar asks himself at the end of the play why he has to go, we know the answer. It is to escape "the enemy within".

A Workshop

Warm-up: **'Samson, Delilah and the Lion'**

1   The whole group moves freely around the space. Everyone should avoid walking in circles and seek to move into unoccupied parts of the room so that if called upon to 'freeze' they will be evenly distributed across the floor area. Freeze the group and ask them to get into pairs.

2   Get each pair to agree who is 'A' and who is 'B'. Demonstrate three images: 'Samson', 'Delilah' and 'The Lion' with simple body images. (Samson might have his arms raised like a strongman, Delilah might be curvaceously seductive, the lion will gesture with its 'claws'). Explain that Samson defeats the

Lion, Delilah defeats Samson, and the Lion defeats Delilah. The analogy of the playground game, 'Scissors, Paper, Stone' is often helpful in explaining this.

3   Get each pair to stand back to back about a metre apart. Everyone selects one of the three images. Everyone is to turn round quickly and form their chosen image when the facilitator says the words "1-2-3-turn". If both images are the same, no-one scores. If one is stronger, that person scores.

4   Repeat the process five times in quick succession.

Note: The usual result is to energise the group amid gales of laughter, while raising the sensitivity of the group to stage images.

'Photography'

1   Get each pair to decide who will be the photographer and who the model.

2   Ask the photographer to close his/her eyes and the model to strike an interesting pose.

3   The photographer is allowed to open his/her eyes for five seconds only while the facilitator counts clearly – "Open-2-3-4-5-Close".

4   The model relaxes his/her pose and the photographer with open eyes has to recreate the image the model has just shown.

5   Repeat with roles reversed. The pairs should begin to feel comfortable looking closely at one another.

'Reflections'

1   Get each pair to face one another. One is the mirror, the other the reflection. They should decide between themselves which will lead a simple movement sequence which the other will copy in mirror image.

2   The facilitator should then try to spot which partner is leading.

Note: this and other exercises in pairs can introduce the idea of the Private/Public 'double act'.

'Public & Private'

1   Get each pair to agree that one will be 'Private', the other 'Public'. Everyone moves around the room as at the start of the session, except that Public must avoid eye contact with everyone else, and Private must seek out eye contact with as many others as possible except their partner.

2   Discuss briefly the implications of this for our understanding of the Public/Private staging convention where Private can see Public but Public cannot see Private.

Exercise 1: **'Unspoken Text'** – Having worked through this preparatory warm-up, choose two of the more confident pairs to improvise an everyday situation involving two characters. The Public characters should pause after each sentence to allow the Private character to say what the Public character is really thinking. The closer the relationship between the two characters the better this exercise usually works.

Exercise 2: **'Four Chairs'**

1   Ask the group to arrange themselves on one side of the room like an audience. Place four similar chairs on the 'stage' in front of them.

2   Ask for volunteers to arrange the chairs, moving any or all of them to make one more important than the others.

3   As soon as each volunteer completes an image, point to each chair asking for the other group members to raise a hand if they think it is the most important. Often there is a division of opinion. If so, ask for reasons for each choice. Stress that there can be as many different reasons as there are people in the room, because everyone who sees the image perceives their own version of it, influenced by their own personal circumstances and perspective.

4   Relate the exercise to the process of seeing a play. Like the chairs, a play can be interpreted in different ways by the different people who see it. Relate this to the differing memories of characters in *Philadelphia, Here I Come!*

Note: in my experience, this exercise has been helpful in explaining the idea of subjectivity.

Exercise 3: '**Playing the Silence**'

1   Choose four actors to read through the draughts scene (in Episode Three, Part I) as it is written with Private interjecting his lines. Stage the scene simply with S.B. and the Canon facing each other at a table, and Public and Private standing a short distance on either side facing the audience. Public should not look at the other characters. Private can look at them directly.

2   Re-run the scene without Private's lines but ask the person who has previously spoken the part to read the lines silently and as close to real time as possible. Agree some simple signal which will allow him to alert the other actors when they should speak their next line. Discuss briefly the effect of allowing the real silence to be heard.

3   Finally, re-run the scene as written and discuss briefly the impact the exercise has had on the collective understanding of the way the silences work, especially in relation to the actors playing S.B. and the Canon.

Note: the same exercise can be done for other scenes, including Kate's visit and the visit of "The boys".

Exercise 4: '**Mendelssohn**'

Play a recording of the first part of the first movement of the Mendelssohn Violin Concerto while reading the relevant dialogue from Episode One. Notice how the music becomes an additional stage direction, indicating the required pace of performance. (Consider this effect in the light of the discussion of *Performances* in Chapter 6.) Now play the second movement while the relevant scene in Part I of Episode Three is read aloud. Note the way that this affects your understanding of the dialogue, especially the Canon's line: "What's that noise?"

Translations

It may seem strange to have discovered the essential truth about playing Friel in Transylvania. But that is how it happened for me. In 2001, I was invited to direct *Translations* for the Hungarian Theatre in Cluj-Napoca, a city in northern Romania that during the Habsburg Empire had been a major centre of Hungarian culture. After the First World War, the region was ceded to Romania and the city's former Habsburg Winter and Summer Theatres became the Romanian and Hungarian Theatres respectively. After the end of the Second World War, Romania fell within the Soviet sphere of influence, and the theatres were made to conform to the socialist model with large permanent drama and opera companies sharing the theatre and presenting their work on alternate nights.

Under the dictatorship of Ceausescu in the 1970s and 1980s, a deliberate effort was made to disperse the Hungarian population throughout Romania and to bring in larger numbers of ethnic Romanians. The Hungarians increasingly were made to feel foreigners in their traditional homeland, but clung to their traditions with tenacity, language being the principle symbol of their identity. When Ceausescu was deposed and executed on Christmas Day in 1989, the resulting coup proved more cosmetic and less far-reaching than in neighbouring countries. As the old shibboleths of Socialism disappeared all along the former Iron Curtain, in Romania these structures proved strangely resilient. In particular, the Hungarian minority nurtured their separate cultural institutions in the face of continuing prejudice from the authorities.

For all these reasons, I was cautious when it came to directing as potentially a political play as *Translations* in Cluj-Napoca, or Koloszvar as it is in Hungarian. I was concerned that I might come under pressure to make it relate specifically to the Romanian context. My hope, which I believe the final production vindicated, was that by avoiding confusion between English-as-English and English-as-Irish, the use of a third language would actually serve to clarify the bi-lingual reality that was being represented on stage. This created a unique challenge for the translator, Erika Mihalycsa, but I was encouraged by the fact that she had a detailed knowledge not only of English and her native Hungarian, but also of Irish – a fact I considered little short of remarkable given the marginalized nature of the Irish language even in Ireland.

An early issue was how best to render the place names that are so central to the play. As can be seen from any modern map of Ireland, the standardisation of Irish names into English took one of two forms – a phonetic approximation of the Irish or a literal translation into English. For example, Carraig na Ri or 'Rock of the King' becomes Kingsrock, while Baile Beag becomes Ballybeg. I was adamant that for the play to work, it would be necessary to preserve this distinction in the Hungarian version, by rendering the translated names into Hungarian. I wanted to convey the sense that the names were being colonised. Erika was unconvinced, expressing in an e-mail to me in January 2001 her concern that "the alterity, the foreignness of the words would be lost". Her solution was to provide both versions for us to experiment with in rehearsal.

Having worked with the Hungarian names for some days, one of the actors complained that the names sounded too natural. I argued that the same could be said by an English-speaking audience of their experience of the original play. So the actor refined his point. The problem was that in Hungarian, to a Hungarian ear, the names sounded too 'beautiful'. The English names had an angularity, an ugliness, which conveyed the process of colonisation much more effectively. And so a consensus emerged for us to retain the English names. My dogmatic preoccupation with the mechanics of translating the play *Translations* had been misplaced. The very nature of translation is so delicate, so unpredictable, that the only practical solution was to explore the ideas in practice on the rehearsal room floor.

The truth of this was reinforced when, by rehearsing *Translations* through the medium of an interpreter, we began to parallel the action of the play. In one scene Captain Lancey, the commander of the British army mapmakers, addresses the people of Ballybeg with the help of Owen as translator. The audience, hearing both the 'Irish' and the 'English' in their own language, are able to appreciate the differences between the translation and the original in a way that most of the participants on stage cannot. Only Manus, Owen's brother, queries the veracity of his rendition. Similarly, in our own rehearsal process, I would try and convey my ideas in clear and simple English, wait for the translation, and then continue with the next idea. But despite the excellence of my interpreter, who was also the production's dramaturg, quite often English-speaking members of the acting company would confide in me that "she did not always say what I said".

This conclusion presumes a number of crucial stages. Each actor that could speak English first heard what I had to say, presumably construing it in their own Hungarian version. Secondly, they heard the interpreter's Hungarian translation, which they then had to relate to their own understanding of my original English. Applying the ideas of George Steiner that were discussed in Chapter 3, that all verbal communication is a form of translation, this suggests a double layer of subjective interpretation. What we had been engaged in, in fact, was an empirical exploration of the principles expressed in Steiner's *After Babel*. As a director, the only way I could respond to this was to try to make myself consciously aware of the vagaries inherent in the process. My command of Hungarian was effectively limited to two phrases – expressed phonetically, "probayuk-meg" and "chinayuk-meg" – "let's try it" and "let's do it"! Emblematic as these ideas may be of the rehearsal process, the fact remained that I was exceptionally dependent on what I saw rather than what I heard. And it was perhaps this that led me (albeit subconsciously) to make increasing use of 'Image Theatre' techniques as the rehearsal period progressed.

'Image Theatre' is the generic name for a collection of exercises developed by the celebrated Brazilian director, Augusto Boal. Concerned principally with using theatre as a means of problem-solving in real-life situations, his work can usefully be applied to fictional situations. He consistently favours the use of images over words on the grounds that images are less open to misinterpretation. In this there seems to be clear common ground with the ideas of George Steiner which, as we saw in Chapter 2, were a strong influence on the development of *Translations*. In the case of my own multi-lingual rehearsal process, I found ritualised gestures and tableaux a useful way occasionally of circumventing the need for words. Actors were able to show me their image of a situation or character rather than describe them verbally.

Once the use of images had been established within the rehearsal room, I began to experiment with more sophisticated 'Image Theatre' techniques. In particular, I used Boal's 'Rainbow of Desire' to explore cardinal moments in the text. This exercise allows a group of actors (or as Boal styles them, 'spectactors', to emphasise their dual role as observers and participants) to create a 'stage-map' of a key protagonist's state of mind at any critical moment in the action. The scene is played through and frozen at the point which is to be explored. Then spectators are asked to illustrate by means of a stage image created using their own bodies any of the things that they believe the protagonist might want to do at that moment. The (actor playing the) protagonist can veto each desire, but only if they are adamant that not even a shred of that desire exists in their (character's) mind at the moment in question. (The parentheses remind us that while Boal works mainly with real situations, we are transposing the technique to a fictional world.)

The effect is to create a multi-layered model of Stanislavskian objectives, with a number of competing objectives being able to coexist at the one time. The scene is then rerun, and at the moment of crisis, the protagonist is permitted to argue with each 'desire'. The effect is to establish in the protagonist's mind an intuitive understanding of their attitude towards each one. The final part of the exercise is for the protagonist to arrange the 'desires' on the stage according to their strength. The resulting image can then be analysed collectively by all present. The sheer complexity of the image often surprises even its creator.

Although it was developed by Boal as a quasi-therapeutic technique, I have found the 'Rainbow of Desire' exercise of immense value in a conventional rehearsal context. The idea which I chose to explore using this technique in *Translations* was Owen's struggle between his native (Irish) and his new (English) world as epitomised by the confrontation with his father in Act Two over the potential impact of the new English names:

> **Owen**   Do you know where the priest lives?
>
> **Hugh**   At Lis na Muc, over near ...
>
> **Owen**   No, he doesn't. Lis na Muc, the Fort of the Pigs, has become Swinefort. And to get to Swinefort you pass through Greencastle and Fair Head and Strandhill and Gort and Whiteplains. And the new school isn't at Poll na gCaorach – it's at Sheepsrock. Will you be able to find your way?

The climax of this encounter is heightened, at least in the actor's mind, by the fact that he has spontaneously translated the last name into English. Shortly before he has used the phonetic transcription "Poolkerry" when listing the agreed names at the request of the young English Lieutenant Yolland, who despite his involvement in the map-making is instrumental in making Owen acknowledge the value of the tradition he is seeking to deny.

Applied to the above scene, the 'Rainbow of Desire' revealed a complex web of emotions, with Owen's mind wracked by a spectrum of intertwined and conflicting objectives. Because of the collaborative nature of the technique, the rest of the acting company were closely involved in the process, with actors representing Owen's different desires within an imagistic stage map of his state of mind. Crucially, because of Boal's strictures on the use of words, all these ideas were conveyed chiefly by means of stage images, temporarily transcending the need for language, translation and interpretation.

Given this explanation of the process, the irony of seeking to describe these image-based 'desires' in words will be apparent. But I offer my own subjective interpretation of them in the spirit of clarifying the way in which the technique operated. One spectator offered the actor playing Owen an image of the affection he felt for his father (we will call this 'love'); another an image of the exasperation he felt (we will call this 'anger'); another an image of the disgust, or perhaps sadness he felt at Hugh's evident addiction to poteen, or maybe this was simply a way of saying that 'it was just the drink talking' (we will call this 'concern'); another showed the desire to remonstrate with the cantankerous old man (we will call this 'disagreement'). The inadequacy of words in interpreting these images will be evident from the circumlocution of the above exposition!

Once the 'desires' had been offered and accepted by the actor playing Owen as being present in the character's mind, he was then given an opportunity to debate (using words) in free improvisation with each one. On the basis of this interaction with them, he then positioned each 'desire' within the climactic moment of the scene under consideration, placing those he felt most strongly close to his own stage position; those he felt least strongly furthest away. The completed image was then opened up for general discussion.

When the various levels of interpretation are taken into account, including the stage relationship between each of the 'desires' and each of the characters, the relationship between the 'desires' themselves, and the added dimension of the audience, the possible readings of the image are legion. And it is important to appreciate the subjective nature of the exercise. Collective analysis revealed, for example, that at least in this actor's mind, there was no immediate threat of Owen venting his anger, but by placing this desire behind Hugh's back and in sight of Yolland, there was a clear indication that he wanted his English friend to understand his exasperation but not to give his father the satisfaction of knowing how far he had been riled. The love Owen felt towards his father was strong, and was blocking his anger. He wanted the audience to have some sense of this love, but not of the concern he felt about his father's drinking which he masked from them with his own body. Yolland, on the other hand, could see this concern, which at the same time prevented him from seeing the 'desire' representing the love Owen felt for his father – too intimate an emotion, perhaps to have shared with his friend. What it revealed to me in the current context was an intuitive sense of how that particular actor saw his role in that particular production context, which was exactly what, as a director, I most needed to know.

There was one other important set of images which had a profound influence on the development of the production, and which underlined the subjective nature of any rehearsal process. On the second day of rehearsal I received a text message from a friend in Belfast on my mobile phone. "Have you seen the news?". It was 11th September 2001. At the end of the session we left the rehearsal room to find most of the theatre staff crowded around a computer mesmerised by the repeated internet images of the Twin Towers. Inevitably, such earth-shattering news affected our work. The world in which we were presenting our play had profoundly changed. While the choice of *Translations* had been inspired by the coexistence in Cluj of two language cultures, the Hungarian and the Romanian, from that day on I became increasingly aware of the growing importance of English to both language groups, and for the same reason that is identified in Friel's play – its effectiveness as a medium for commerce. The destruction of the World Trade Center seemed cruelly to underline this fact. In Transylvania in the shadow of recent history with Internet Cafés on every corner, our production of *Translations*, when it opened in early October, became ultimately about the colonial capacity of the English language.

Chatting with the actors outside the rehearsal room, it became clear that for them, the great puzzlement of the piece was that the Irish let their language die. Although small pockets of the *Gaeltacht* survive today, the Irish experience bears no relation to the tenacious hold that Hungarian-speakers in Romania retain on their language and the culture and traditions that flow from it. Their conclusion, which I am inclined to share, is that whereas Ceausescu sought pro-actively to suppress minority languages, the English found that commercial incentive contributed in large measure to the Irish themselves allowing their hitherto majority language to fall into disuse.

It is possible to describe this analysis in gravitational terms, since language is clearly one of the major ways in which cultural gravity expresses itself. If the gravitational power of the English language at the height of the British Empire exerted such a terrific force, how much greater is that influence now that the cultural mass of the English language has expanded to include the United States? The forces of cultural gravity at work in Inishowen included the native Irish (stronger through proximity than mass) and the English (Dublin and London exerting a more or less equal pull). In Cluj/Kolozsvar the effect of the relative pull of Bucharest and Budapest is obviously influenced by each individual's mother tongue. For those whose first language is Hungarian, however, the proximity and mass of Budapest ensures its dominance, the border between Romania and Hungary notwithstanding. It was no surprise, therefore, that when my production of *Translations* toured it was to Budapest and not to the Romanian capital. But overwhelming both more local allegiances, the cultural mass of English appears to be the strongest force of all. Thus the Romanian experience is increasingly coming to reflect Friel's own analysis of the Irish that "we are no longer even West Britons; we are East Americans".

As I lived and worked within a Hungarian minority in a Romanian city I began to have a stronger sense of the power of language in defining identity, and how as Hugh remarks in *Translations*: "it is not the literal past, the 'facts' of history, that shape us, but images of the past embodied in language". This accords with an earlier comment of Friel's, that:

> in some ways the inherited images of 1916 or 1690 control and rule our lives much more profoundly than the historical truth of what happened on those two occasions. The complication of that problem is how do we come to terms with it using an English language".

The Hungarians in Koloszvar were at least relieved of that peculiar 20th-century Irish dilemma.

One last revelation awaited me. During a late rehearsal, to lighten the mood, I ran the whole play asking the actors to adopt a different style for each scene. They had some awareness of O'Casey, for instance, so it was natural to ask for the final scene between Hugh and Jimmy Jack to be played with conscious reference to Joxer and Captain Boyle, whose own final scene in *Juno and the Paycock* it so closely resembles. When Hugh enters reciting Latin poetry in Act Two, on a whim I suggested that the actors play the scene in the style of Friel's great influence, Anton Chekhov. Suddenly the fine old actor, Csiki Andras, who was playing Hugh, transformed himself into a perfect Chekhovian professor. This has left two main impressions: the extent to which he had so totally and effectively assimilated the Russian tradition through decades of Soviet influence; and the clear distinction in playing styles between the delicate naturalism that is required of true Chekhov, and the heightened realism that characterises Friel's own work. Ballybeg is saturated with a powerful theatricality which far from being a weakness is its great defining strength. The distance provided by my Romanian production allowed me the objectivity to understand this to the full.

A Workshop

Warm-up: **'Chinese Movements'**

1.   Depending on the size of the group, divide into a number of smaller units of at least eight and no more than ten people. Get each group to stand as if in a bus queue facing the same wall.

2.   Standing at that wall, explain the rules of the game as follows
      – you will illustrate a simple movement sequence to the person
      at the back of each line, who will then tap the shoulder of the
      next person in line to get them to turn round.

3.   The first person will then show the next person the same
      movement sequence and so on down the line. Each sequence
      will be shown to each person twice.

4.   The last person will then show the whole group what they
      have seen, followed by the first person or the facilitator's
      original version.

5.   The whole group then discuss any differences and the reason
      for them. Usually there are radical differences, influenced by
      the personalities of all the participants and their desire to
      impose meaning.

Note: The best sequences are as neutral as possible and consist of
        about three distinct components. The relevance of this exercise
        to *Translations*, with its preoccupation with non-verbal
        communication and the "inner core" can then be opened up to
        general discussion. The exercise can also be seen as a metaphor
        for the erosion of meaning as language passes from generation
        to generation.

'Stage Maps'

1.   Explain that the floor of the room corresponds to the
      geographical area where you happen to be working. Ask
      everyone to place him/herself on the map according to where
      he/she was born. If they were born outside the area they should
      stand on the edge of the space nearest the place they want to
      represent. E.g. if they were born to the north of the defined
      space, they should stand against the north wall.

2.   Repeat the exercise for where each person lives now. Then
      ask each person to say a phrase that they associate with the
      place they are standing with the strongest possible accent.

3.   Briefly discuss the idea of diversity of voice, language and
      accent as it affects the specific group.

Exercise 1: **'Two Tribes'** (this exercise requires two adjacent spaces)

1.   After an initial discussion of the difference in the formation of vowels, and voiced and unvoiced consonants, divide the group in two. Place each group in a different room.

2.   Ask each group to envisage a world in which the language consists only of vowels or consonants (one for each group). They should think of a name for their tribe, individual names for themselves, and they should also devise a tribal rite or ceremony. Finally they should agree on one member of their group to be an ambassador who will visit the other tribe. Setting up the exercise should be done in English. After that the group should only communicate in their own new language!

3.   After a suitable interval, the tutor arranges for the exchange of ambassadors, and again after a suitable interval, for their safe return.

4.   The ambassador tries to convey in his/her own language the customs/nature of the other group to his/her own group.

5.   When this has run its course, declare the exercise over and bring the groups back together to discuss their findings. Usually (but not always) the vowel culture is more peaceful, the consonant culture more vibrant!

6.   Finally, discuss the exercise in relation to the themes of *Translations*.

Note: A subtler additional or alternative exercise is to characterise the two tribes by languages consisting only of voiced (B, D, Z, etc.) and unvoiced (P, T, S, etc.) consonants. The results of this variant are much less predictable!

Exercise 2: **'Rhubarb, Rhubarb!'**

1.   Work out a simple staging of the end of Act One of *Translations*, with the Irish speakers on one side and the English officers on the other. Having assigned parts, have everyone read through the scene as written.

2.   Now rerun the scene but substitute all the words you think are spoken in Irish with the repeated word "Rhubarb", or some

other gobbledygook of the group's own choice. It is important that concentration is retained and the expressiveness of the characters remain the same.

3. Now repeat the exercise substituting similarly meaningless sounds for all the words you think are spoken in English. Bear in mind, that there may be some phrases where the intended language is not clear and some speeches which are spoken partly in Irish and partly in English. Discussing these options will help clarify the final playing of the scene.

4. Finally, rerun the full text as written. Discuss any changes you notice between the first and final version.

Note: the exercise can also be applied to the love scene (Act Two, Scene II).

Exercise 3: **'Comparing Translations'**

1. Select a short scene (no more than a page) with three characters from three versions of Chekhov's *Three Sisters*: Friel's, Frank McGuinness' and any other English translation.

2. Assign each role to a different actor and get them to read the passage, each working from a different translation. Discuss how this sounds. How distinctive is the language of each character/translation? Extend the discussion to consider the writer's intention in each case. For Friel, rendering the words in a distinctive Irish style of English is crucial. McGuinness (whom Friel selected to write the screenplay of *Dancing at Lughnasa* and who has great sympathy with his work) was writing specifically for three actresses, the three daughters of the great old Irish actor, Cyril Cusack. Are these intentions evident in the way the different texts sound when read aloud?

3. Reread each version with each actor using the same text. Does this clarify the audience's understanding of each author's intention? Why might a director choose each version for a specific production of the play?

Exercise 4: **'The Rainbow of Desire'** – You may like to experiment with the Boal 'Rainbow of Desire' exercise as it is described above.

Other suitable scenes include the confrontation between Maire and Manus just before the English soldiers enter in Act One, the exchange between Owen and Manus at the end of Act One, the Lancey scene and the Doalty and Owen scene in Act Three. You can choose to 'rainbow' either character in each case according to the following checklist:

1. Run the scene, ending with an agreed point of climax.

2. Ask the 'spectactors' (see p.56) to show images of possible things the protagonist might want to do at that moment (however much or however little).

3. Allow the actor playing the protagonist to accept or veto each suggested image. Accepted 'desires' remain at the back of the stage.

4. Ask the protagonist to illustrate any missing 'desires', and ask for 'spectactor' volunteers (see above) to represent these.

5. Re-run the scene and allow the protagonist briefly to debate with each desire in turn arguing against them.

6. Re-run the scene a final time and have all the desires gather round the protagonist competing for his/her attention (like voices in his/her head). The protagonist silences the 'desires' in turn by placing a hand on their shoulders, but only when clear how strongly he or she feels them.

7. The protagonist then arranges the 'desires' anywhere on the stage according to how strongly they affect him/her in relation to his/her own final position in the scene before returning to that position.

8. Finally, the group analyse the resulting image according to how the desires are arranged in relation to the protagonist, and other characters in the scene, each other and the audience.

Dancing at Lughnasa

Unlike the immediate experience of directing *Philadelphia, Here I Come!* and *Translations*, my encounters with *Dancing at Lughnasa* have been more vicarious but ultimately no less intense. In recent years, a number of groups of my own students have explored key scenes from the play and each have revealed their own insights, but my main insights have flowed from the production directed by Conall Morrison at the Lyric Theatre, Belfast, in my time there as Associate Director. Morrison's production was unusual in that it was wholly independent of Patrick Mason's original Abbey version that was effectively franchised throughout the world. Morrison was able to work in Belfast, closer to Friel's imaginative Donegal heartland than Dublin, on a distinctive interpretation of the play.

My most lasting impression of seeing the original production was the contribution made by each of the five actresses in creating such memorable and richly imagined manifestations of Friel's Mundy sisters. As I wrote in *Theatre Ireland* magazine:

> If the principal preoccupation of the Victorian theatre can be said to have been the representation of reality, the main challenge facing the modern theatre is ... how to present *un*reality. Friel ... excels at discovering devices which allow actors to explore with their audiences a world of possibilities beyond the boundaries of reality ... [But] whereas in [*Philadelphia, Here I Come!*] Private Gar lives inside Public Gar's imagination and is able to comment on the 'real' action, in *Dancing at Lughnasa* the narrator ... inhabits the real world with the audience and looks in on the action with us ... It would have been all too easy for the action ... to have had a kind of misty, sentimental quality ... In fact a superb set of rugged and carefully detailed performances ensure that we are given a very direct and uncompromising picture of the people and ideas that give substance to the play ... [The director, Patrick] Mason developed a kind of heightened ordinariness, where everyday action assumed the status of ritual. Kitchen chores and the knitting of socks were acted out with distinctive precision ... The result was that the fullness of Friel's characters were given life, but we were always aware that we were seeing the action at one remove, through the mind of the narrator ... The women in particular each succeeded in asserting their different natures. Frances Tomelty's brittle school teacher Kate, Anita Reeve's fun-loving and gauche Maggie, Brid Brennan's thoughtful and alluring Agnes, Brid Ni Neachtain's simple but assertive Rose, Catherine Byrnes's romantic yet responsible Chris.

The Lyric production provided the opportunity for five new actors to rediscover the play in partnership with Morrison, a director thoroughly familiar with Friel's world but coming to the play for the first time. His reading of the play eschewed the sense of distance that I had perceived in Patrick Mason's production in favour of a visceral intensity that fully realised the harsh reality of the lives these brave women led. As he puts it himself, the eponymous dance "isn't nought to sixty". It doesn't come out of nowhere. It is latently seething from the start of the play. While this sense of volatility was certainly in the first production, in Morrison's account of the play it was even more highly charged.

Nor did he see the play as a projection of Michael's memory. As we have already observed in relation to *Philadelphia, Here I Come!* in Chapter 2, the idea of a 'memory play' is problematic when the audience see scenes that the rememberer cannot have witnessed. And Morrison was clear that Michael, the child, could not have understood the complexity of his aunts' collective psyche, even had he observed the scenes the play shares with us and not been playing outside. What we see is therefore the construct of an adult mind, far removed from the immediate reality of the displayed action.

Morrison recalls one episode during the run of the play that made him aware of the differences between his production and the one that was enjoying an extended run in the West End. Eileen McCloskey who played Chris in the Belfast production fell ill, and had to be replaced at short notice for some performances by Maggie Cronin who had appeared in the London production. Maggie reported her immense sense of dislocation at finding herself in such a radically different interpretation of the same play. She found it difficult to connect Morrison's hard-edged reading with the rose-tinted version she had experienced in the West End. The role of Agnes was also a revelation, Paula McFetridge's performance revealing an inner passion which I cannot recall seeing in Brid Brennan, although when I read the text now it seems self-evident on the page.

Morrison acknowledges the importance in coming to an under-standing of the world of the play of hearing archive recordings at the Ulster Folk and Transport Museum of real Glenties women who grew up in the same period as the Mundy sisters. Their raw, untrammelled use of a distinctive mid-Donegal English was almost impossible for him to understand, but it captured what T.S. Eliot has called "the auditory imagination". It evoked a powerful sense of place. Interestingly, in relation to the theme of *Translations*, he remembers it having much stronger resonances with the Irish language than is evident in today's (post-Marconi!) Donegal English. The accumulative influence of decades of radio and television broadcasting has accelerated the "erosion" of the local voice that Lieutanant Yolland in *Translations* foresaw.

Morrison's process underlines the inescapable significance in theatre of interpretation – from both the actors' and the director's perspective. Undoubtedly this can work both for and against the integrity of the text, but to deny its significance, as Friel has done, is akin to King Canute seeking to turn back the tide. The secret of Morrison's success lies in his commitment to playing each scene for the truth. This requires a totally honest engagement with the text so that it will reveal itself. The director, he argues, cannot hope for success in simply seeking to impose a generalised atmosphere or mood.

A Workshop

Warm-up: **'Character Walks'**

1. Ask the group to walk around the room so that they fill the space evenly. They should avoid walking in circles, and look for space as it becomes unoccupied.

2. Ask everyone to find a walk that is based on leading with a particular part of the body (e.g. chin, elbow, chest, hip, groin)?

3. Ask if this suggests anything about the character they might be conveying to an audience.

4. Ask them to imagine a character from the play and over a count of ten to adapt their walk to that of the character.

5. Ask them to vary the walk in a number of simple ways – e.g. the character walking slowly or walking fast, or the character stopping to admire the view. Ask participants really to see the view and store it away in their memory for future discussion.

6.   Now gather with the group in one corner of the room and ask each group member one by one to walk across the room from the corner on your left to the corner on your right (assuming a rectangular room) while the others watch. The whole group should then cross the room trying to copy each walk as it is demonstrated.

7.   Discuss which characteristics most define each walk. Do people lead with particular parts of their body? Is their natural gait slow or fast?

Note: Bear in mind that this kind of scrutiny can be an uncomfortable experience for many people. Be prepared to discuss this discomfort and its relationship to the demands of performance.

Exercise 1: **'The Dance'**

1.   In groups of five, ask each group member to select one of the Mundy sisters and to find a walk for the character (as demonstrated in the above warm-up).

2.   Now mark through the stage directions for the dance concentrating entirely on maintaining the physical sense of the character that this exercise suggests.

3.   Now freely improvise a movement sequence keeping the basic shape of the dance from the play, but to a highly energised section of Stravinsky's *Rite of Spring*. Repeat with any suitable Irish dance music (*The Mason's Apron* as specified by Friel, if this is available). Try and maintain the order in which characters enter and leave the dance, but no other details need be preserved.

4.   Discuss the experience. What effect did the timing of the entrance to and exit from the scene have on each performer's sense of character?

Exercise 2: **'Tableaux'**

1.   In groups of 6-8, get one group member to create a tableau using all other members of the group which represents a crucial moment in any story. The creator of the image should have a

clear idea of who each character is, but convey only the desired body image to each actor by illustrating it (including facial expression) to the person who is to represent that character. If necessary they can mould the bodies of the other participants as if sculpting the image.

2. The tutor/facilitator should then invite one of the characters to step out of the scene and to tell the story of the scene from the perspective of the character they represent as if that character was still part of the scene.

3. Then get the creator of the picture to tell the story they had in mind and compare this with the first story.

4. Discuss the implications of this exercise for the narrative conventions in *Dancing at Lughnasa*.

Exercise 3: '**Marowicz Madness**! – The American director Charles Marowicz in his book *The Other Way* explores a number of techniques aimed at going beyond the conventional psychology of traditional Stanislavskian naturalism. Given what has been said enough about the suppressed passions of the Mundy sisters, the following exercise which is based on Marowicz's ideas, may prove useful in allowing actors access to the subconscious reality of the various characters. It should only be attempted after a thorough warm-up, in a suitable, 'drama-friendly' space, and with a group who are familiar with one another and the drama method.

1. In a circle, ask each group member to pronounce the vowel sound 'ah' in a distinctive way. One may express surprise, another fear, another excitement, and so on. Repeat, if time allows for the vowel sound 'oh'.

2. Select a highly charged section of text involving a number of characters. Read it through together.

3. Ask each actor to express the objectives of his/her character as a desire, i.e. "I want to …" followed by the appropriate verb. There should be a series of such short phrases for each character (ideally four or five) indicating how each actor's objectives shift during the scene.

4. Play the scene (off book) with each actor substituting the short phrases for the original dialogue.

5. Now ask each actor to reduce each phrase to a single key word. Play the scene as before using only these words.

6. Now ask each actor to reduce these single words to single vowel sounds that appear in the words. Rerun the scene repeatedly using only these sounds encouraging the actors to release the animalistic emotions that underlie the text. The result should be vocal but contain a raw emotional power. Some participants will really engage with this, and may get quite physical. Interrupt the exercise if there seems to be any risk of actual physical harm, but the exercise works most effectively when the actors can free themselves from normal constraints.

7. Finally rerun the text, allowing any emotional discoveries to emerge organically.

Note: One objective might be: "I want to escape". The keyword would be 'escape'. The vowel would be the 'a' in escape, which like most dipthongs is capable of infinite distortion and expressive range.

6

A Matter of Interpretation

"Words don't work," exclaimed the eminent English theatre director, Declan Donnellan. "Trying to express in words what we want or feel is like knitting a scarf with tree trunks." It would seem that Friel and Donnellan have both arrived at a similar conclusion through a lifetime of experience in their respective crafts. To be more precise, what Hamlet describes as "words, words, words" go only a little way by themselves to communicate theatrical truth. The missing element we may describe as 'interpretation'.

Given that a recurrent theme in Friel's writing for the stage has been the subjective nature of experience there is an irony in his often expressed indifference for directors. This makes insufficient allowance for the fact that any play text, however definitive, can only reach the stage through the mediation of interpreters, be they directors, designers or actors. One could understand it if Friel was basing his attitude towards directors on the authorial tradition of directing which prevails in Germany and much of continental Europe where the directorial 'konzept' often treats the work of the dramatist as a mere pretext for the director's creativity. But the approach of most directors in the English-speaking theatre, and certainly those who have worked most closely with Friel, continues to accord the realisation of the writer's intention supreme importance. In my own experience of working with Friel's work, the process of directing a play has been an organic and collaborative one that consisted in a shared discovery of the text by director and actors. And yet Friel persists in minimising his experience of the rich creative partnerships he has enjoyed with the likes of Hilton Edwards, Joe Dowling and Patrick Mason.

Speaking with the journalist Ciaran Carty in 1980 he outlined his expectations of a director:

> The dramatist ought to be able to exercise a complete control over the realisation of his characters. The director can bring an objective view to the script that a writer can't have. But I'm very doubtful about the whole idea of a director interpreting a play in any kind of way that's distinctive to him. A good director homes in on what the core of the play is about and realizes that and becomes self-effacing in the process. A director is like the conductor of an orchestra and the actors are the musicians. They are all there to play the score as it is written.

This reiterates the position set out clearly in his 'Self-Portrait' in 1972 in which he acknowledges the fact that without interpreters a script is like "a kite without wind, a boat waiting for a tide", but sets stringent guidelines about the nature of this interpretation:

> I look to the director and the actors to interpret that score exactly as written. It is not their function to rewrite, or to cut, or to extend. It is their function, their only function – and an enormously difficult one – to interpret what is given to them. And I use the analogy of the orchestral score with deliberation because I have never known a conductor who would even dream of tampering with the shape of a symphony.

None of this is inconsistent with my own understanding of the director's role, but by the 1990s, his position has hardened still further. In an interview with Mel Gussow in 1991 for the *New York Times* Magazine he is quoted as saying:

> I want a director to call rehearsals, to make sure the actors are there on time and to get them to speak clearly and distinctly … I've no interest whatever in his concept or interpretation. I think it's almost a bogus career.

In 1999, in notes written for his 70th birthday Festival, the comparison is no longer with the conductor of an orchestra but with the conductor of a bus, which we used to consider important "until one day we realized that the conductor was altogether superfluous".

Sadly, the critical reception of the premieres of both *Molly Sweeney* (1994) and *Give Me Your Answer, Do!* (1997), both of which Friel directed himself, established that however hard it was to define, the director did have a role which the writer alone could not fulfil.

For me, the key to understanding the director's role, apart from fulfilling the vital function of providing an outside eye, flows from precisely the musical analogy that Friel himself employs. It is all about the effective deployment of resources or, as musicians say, of 'forces'. The parts of an orchestral score may well be fixed, but the conductor must understand the potential and also the limitations of each instrumentalist and achieve a collective response to the score that allows all these different personalities to work in concert. The stage director, however, is dealing with performers who are by definition their own instrument, and the process is inevitably much more mercurial. In short, the director must negotiate with exactly those 'privacies' and that inner core which are the subject of so much of Friel's writing.

In his diary for 31st January 1977, Friel asks:

> Is there an anti-art element in theatre in that it doesn't speak to the individual in his absolute privacy and isolation but addresses him as an audience? And if it is possible to receive the dramatist and apprehend him as an individual, is the art being confronted on a level that wasn't intended?

Later that year (on 16th December) he observes that:

> The dramatist has to recycle his experience through the pressure-cooker of his imagination. He has to present this new reality to a public – 300 diverse imaginations come together with no more serious intent than the casual wish to be 'entertained'. And he has got to forge those 300 imaginations into one perceiving faculty, dominate and condition them so that they become attuned to the tonality of the transmission and consequently to its meaning ... But to talk of 'meaning' is inaccurate. We say "What is the play about?" with more accuracy than "What does a play mean?" Because we don't go to art for meaning. We go to it for perceptions of new adjustments and new arrangements.

Taken together, these comments illustrate Friel's exceptional understanding of the unique intimacy and subjectivity of the performance process. But the desire to harness all these disparate imaginations is surely misplaced. If every member of an audience comes out of a performance all with exactly the same perception of the play, has it not then failed in some important respect in not having communicated to them uniquely as individuals.

It is difficult not to have sympathy for a dramatist's desire for ownership and control over his work. Friel has said that "art is fundamentally and primarily an attempt to give some kind of structure to your own life and your own beliefs and your own confusions", and it is clear that for Friel his writing is immensely personal. But the true power of live theatre, is to allow such intimate and passionate truths to be shared with a whole audience. Expressive actors and a sensitive director are necessary to allow this to happen, even if their contribution is inert and impotent without the vital input of the creative writer. Their subjective input provides an essential catalyst for the release of the subjective response of each audience member.

Friel's continuing fascination with these issues is evident in his play about the Czech composer Janácek, *Performances*, which was premiered at the Gate Theatre as part of the 2003 Dublin Theatre Festival. The one-word plural title provides the first clue to the play's connections with *Translations* and the continuing influence of George Steiner, whom Friel acknowledges explicitly in the programme. In *Performances*, however, he takes the idea of translation to a new level, exploring the remarkable capacity of music directly to communicate emotions and the most visceral of ideas.

From the emotional intensity of Mendelssohn's Violin Concerto in *Philadelphia, Here I Come!* to the liberating energy of the ceilidh music in *Dancing at Lughnasa* the importance of music throughout Friel's canon is self-evident. In *Performances*, however, he pushes the metaphorical significance of music as the most direct means of emotional communication to new heights, and has Janácek remark:

> Thank God that my first language was music ... The people who huckster in words merely report on feeling. We speak feeling.

And the musicality of Friel's own work has drawn comment from both actors and directors. As Rosaleen Linehan, the finest living Dublin actress, has observed:

> This is what for me Brian Friel presents you as an actor. Music first. The learning of the script and the text is so vital. Not just the words, his punctuation, and his semicolons and his dots-dots-dots … And his dashes! These have to be learned as precisely as the actual words on the page … At your peril do you move off it. It's like orchestration – there's duets, there's trios, there's quintets, there's solos, and each has to be taken on that level and each of these has to be performed as cleanly, as unselfishly really, as possible … I don't think his plays attract selfish playing.

Patrick Mason, the first director of *Dancing at Lughnasa* echoes these sentiments when he reports Friel's own advice to the players:

> … one line provokes the next … If you inflect the line slightly wrong it will not provoke the next. Therefore the music of the language is extremely precise and I think that is one of the most demanding aspects, this acuteness of ear to the poise of language.

As Mason goes on to add himself:

> There is that precision, absolutely. I think that firm, extraordinary line he gives you, a musical line, is tremendous support in performance. I remember Catherine Byrne saying that … if you followed the shape of it and rhythm of it, it led you to it. It was that strong a thing.

Joe Dowling, a director who has been associated with a large number of Friel premieres amplifies the point, addressing the necessary tension between authorial intent and directorial intuition:

> Directors who see Friel's work as a way of making their own theatrical statements without taking very careful note of the nuances of the text will inevitably do considerable damage to the concise and accurate theatrical imagination which is always evident. It is vital for the director to approach the text of any Friel play with scrupulous attention to detail. The way of

producing the play is always to be found within the work itself. It rarely requires extraneous production ideas. The director has to listen to the music of the text. The actor can often find his clues to the characterisation in the dialogue, not only of his own character but of others. Friel's characters are always rooted in a detailed psychological reality and however heightened the language may be, it is ultimately in that area of emotional truth that the impact will be made on the audience.

But he goes on to say:

This is not to suggest that a director is not an essential ingredient in every production. Rather it affirms the crucial and delicate nature of the relationship between writer and director. Without a strong director shaping each scene, finding the correct pace and rhythm for each character, dictating a sense of momentum which the play requires, then plays may not realise their potential. Actors cannot find that objective realisation of a scene without the careful and intelligent reading of the text by a director who respects the text … To play the music of the text as clearly as the writer has composed it must always be the over-riding objective of any production of a Friel play.

The musical motif assumes special relevance in the case of *Performances* in which the idea of music itself is explicitly addressed.

We toyed in Chapter 4 with comparisons between Friel and Shakespeare. In that respect, *Performances* is surely the Friel counterpart to *The Tempest* – a profound reflection on the artist's own 'rough magic'. In its form, it represents yet another development of the experimental theatricality that was discussed in Chapter 2. In *Performances*, the composer Janácek appears as a ghost-like presence. Just as Kamila, the woman with whom Janácek became fixated in later life is described as his dream music "made carnal", so the character of Janácek is the embodiment of his lingering reputation. Superficially, comparisons with Hugh Leonard's *Da* and *Love in the Title* come to mind. But whereas the spectral presences in Leonard's plays can be understood as manifestations of their central protagonist's imagination, Janácek's presence cannot be explained away as existing only in the mind of Anezka, the PhD student who is seeking to understand Janácek's life through his letters, because the members of the string quartet who are so tangibly and audibly an embodiment of Janácek's music, see him too.

The play also provides further insight into Friel's stance on the process of biography, which we explored in Chapter 1:

> "There must be a connection between the private life and the public work," insists Anezka.
> "You'd learn so much more by just listening to the music," responds Janacek.

When later in the play Anezka insists that the literal meaning that Janácek expresses in his hundreds of love letters must be truer than any metaphorical meaning he might seek to imply, Friel has Janácek reply as follows:

> Not truer, Anezka. No, no, not truer. Yes, both readings can coexist – why not? Be held in a kind of equilibrium. Even be seen to illuminate one another. But finally, Anezka, finally – all this pretty agitation aside – the work's the thing. That must be insisted on.

For all this insistence, there is a sense that in *Performances*, Friel has given ground. The relentless fascination of audiences and academics in the relationship between the author and his work has spun its spell. Just as Janácek seems ultimately to be have been bewitched by the attention of outsiders, so Friel seems to be gradually succumbing to that 'necessary uncertainty', that sharing of control, which is the inevitable result of working within a collaborative medium. Interpretation.

Further Reading

By Brian Friel

Brian Friel, *Plays 1* (Faber, London, 1996) (includes *Philadelphia, Here I Come!, The Freedom of the City, Living Quarters, Aristocrats, Faith Healer* and *Translations*)

Brian Friel, *Plays 2* (Faber, London, 1999) (includes *Dancing at Lughnasa, Fathers and Sons, Making History, Wonderful Tennessee* and *Molly Sweeney*)

Christopher Murray (Ed.), *Brian Friel – Essays, Diaries, Interviews: 1964-1999* (Faber, London, 1999)

About Brian Friel

Richard Pine, *The Diviner* (University College Press, Dublin, 1999)

Elmer Andrews, *The Art of Brian Friel* (MacMillan, London, 1995)

Anthony Roche, *Contemporary Irish Drama* (Gill & MacMillan, London 1994)

Lionel Pilkington, *Theatre and the State in Twentieth-Century Ireland* (Routledge, London 2001)

Tony Coult, *About Friel* (Faber, London, 2003)

GREENWICH EXCHANGE BOOKS

Greenwich Exchange Student Guides are critical studies of major or contemporary serious writers in English and selected European languages. The series is for the student, the teacher and 'common readers' and is an ideal resource for libraries. The *Times Educational Supplement* praised these books, saying, "The style of these guides has a pressure of meaning behind it. Students should learn from that ... If art is about selection, perception and taste, then this is it."

(ISBN prefix 1-871551- applies)
The series includes:
W.H. Auden by Stephen Wade (36-6)
Honoré de Balzac by Wendy Mercer (48-X)
William Blake by Peter Davies (27-7)
The Brontës by Peter Davies (24-2)
Robert Browning by John Lucas (59-5)
Samuel Taylor Coleridge by Andrew Keanie (64-1)
Joseph Conrad by Martin Seymour-Smith (18-8)
William Cowper by Michael Thorn (25-0)
Charles Dickens by Robert Giddings (26-9)
John Donne by Sean Haldane (23-4)
Emily Dickinson by Marnie Pomeroy (68-4)
Ford Madox Ford by Anthony Fowles (63-3)
Robert Frost by Warren Hope (70-6)
Thomas Hardy by Sean Haldane (35-1)
Seamus Heaney by Warren Hope (37-4)
Philip Larkin by Warren Hope (35-8)
Laughter in the Dark – The Plays of Joe Orton by Arthur Burke (56-0)
Philip Roth by Paul McDonald (72-2)
Shakespeare's *Macbeth* by Matt Simpson (69-2)
Shakespeare's *Othello* by Matt Simpson (71-4)
Shakespeare's *The Tempest* by Matt Simpson (75-7)
Shakespeare's Non-Dramatic Poetry by Martin Seymour-Smith (22-6)
Shakespeare's Sonnets by Martin Seymour-Smith (38-2)
Tobias Smollett by Robert Giddings (21-8)
Alfred, Lord Tennyson by Michael Thorn (20-X)
William Wordsworth by Andrew Keanie (57-9)

OTHER GREENWICH EXCHANGE BOOKS

Paperback unless otherwise stated.

Shakespeare's Sonnets

Martin Seymour-Smith

Martin Seymour-Smith's outstanding achievement lies in the field of literary biography and criticism. In 1963 he produced his comprehensive edition, in the old spelling, of *Shakespeare's Sonnets* (here revised and corrected by himself and Peter Davies in 1998). With its landmark introduction and its brilliant critical commentary on each sonnet, it was praised by William Empson and John Dover Wilson. Stephen Spender said of him "I greatly admire Martin Seymour-Smith for the independence of his views and the great interest of his mind"; and both Robert Graves and Anthony Burgess described him as the leading critic of his time. His exegesis of the *Sonnets* remains unsurpassed.

2001 • 194 pages • ISBN 1-871551-38-2

English Language Skills

Vera Hughes

If you want to be sure, (as a student, or in your business or personal life,) that your written English is correct, this book is for you. Vera Hughes' aim is to help you remember the basic rules of spelling, grammar and punctuation. 'Noun', 'verb', 'subject', 'object' and 'adjective' are the only technical terms used. The book teaches the clear, accurate English required by the business and office world. It coaches acceptable current usage and makes the rules easier to remember.

Vera Hughes was a civil servant and is a trainer and author of training manuals.

2002 • 142 pages • ISBN 1-871551-60-9

LITERARY CRITICISM

The Author, the Book and the Reader

Robert Giddings

This collection of essays analyses the effects of changing technology and the attendant commercial pressures on literary styles and subject matter. Authors covered include Charles Dickens, Tobias George Smollett, Mark Twain, Dr Johnson and John le Carré.

1991 • 220 pages • illustrated • ISBN 1-871551-01-3

Liar! Liar!: Jack Kerouac – Novelist
R.J. Ellis
The fullest study of Jack Kerouac's fiction to date. It is the first book to devote an individual chapter to every one of his novels. *On the Road, Visions of Cody* and *The Subterraneans* are reread in-depth, in a new and exciting way. *Visions of Gerard* and *Doctor Sax* are also strikingly reinterpreted, as are other daringly innovative writings, like 'The Railroad Earth' and his "try at a spontaneous *Finnegan's Wake*" – *Old Angel Midnight*. Neglected writings, such as *Tristessa* and *Big Sur*, are also analysed, alongside better-known novels such as *Dharma Bums* and *Desolation Angels*.
R.J. Ellis is Senior Lecturer in English at Nottingham Trent University.
1999 • 295 pages • ISBN 1-871551-53-6

BIOGRAPHY

The Good That We Do
John Lucas
John Lucas' book blends fiction, biography and social history in order to tell the story of his grandfather, Horace Kelly. Headteacher of a succession of elementary schools in impoverished areas of London, 'Hod' Kelly was also a keen cricketer, a devotee of the music hall, and included among his friends the great Trade Union leader, Ernest Bevin. In telling the story of his life, Lucas has provided a fascinating range of insights into the lives of ordinary Londoners from the First World War until the outbreak of the Second World War. Threaded throughout is an account of such people's hunger for education, and of the different ways government, church and educational officialdom ministered to that hunger. *The Good That We Do* is both a study of one man and of a period when England changed, drastically and forever.
John Lucas is Professor of English at Nottingham Trent University and is a poet and critic.
2001 • 214 pages • ISBN 1-871551-54-4

In Pursuit of Lewis Carroll
Raphael Shaberman
Sherlock Holmes and the author uncover new evidence in their investigations into the mysterious life and writing of Lewis Carroll. They examine published works by Carroll that have been overlooked by previous commentators. A newly discovered poem, almost certainly by Carroll, is published here.
Amongst many aspects of Carroll's highly complex personality, this book explores his relationship with his parents, numerous child friends, and the formidable Mrs Liddell, mother of the immortal Alice. Raphael Shaberman

was a founder member of the Lewis Carroll Society and a teacher of autistic children.
1994 • 118 pages • illustrated • ISBN 1-871551-13-7

Musical Offering
Yolanthe Leigh
In a series of vivid sketches, anecdotes and reflections, Yolanthe Leigh tells the story of her growing up in the Poland of the 1930s and the Second World War. These are poignant episodes of a child's first encounters with both the enchantments and the cruelties of the world; and from a later time, stark memories of the brutality of the Nazi invasion, and the hardships of student life in Warsaw under the Occupation. But most of all this is a record of inward development; passages of remarkable intensity and simplicity describe the girl's response to religion, to music, and to her discovery of philosophy.
Yolanthe Leigh was formerly a Lecturer in Philosophy at Reading University.
2000 • 57 pages • ISBN: 1-871551-46-3

Norman Cameron
Warren Hope
Norman Cameron's poetry was admired by W.H. Auden, celebrated by Dylan Thomas and valued by Robert Graves. He was described by Martin Seymour-Smith as, "one of ... the most rewarding and pure poets of his generation ..." and is at last given a full length biography. This eminently sociable man, who had periods of darkness and despair, wrote little poetry by comparison with others of his time, but always of a consistently high quality – imaginative and profound.
2000 • 221 pages • illustrated • ISBN 1-871551-05-6

POETRY

Adam's Thoughts in Winter
Warren Hope
Warren Hope's poems have appeared from time to time in a number of literary periodicals, pamphlets and anthologies on both sides of the Atlantic. They appeal to lovers of poetry everywhere. His poems are brief, clear, frequently lyrical, characterised by wit, but often distinguished by tenderness. The poems gathered in this first book-length collection counter the brutalising ethos of contemporary life, speaking of and for the virtues of modesty, honesty and gentleness in an individual, memorable way.
2000 • 47 pages • ISBN 1-871551-40-4

Baudelaire: Les Fleurs du Mal

Translated by F.W. Leakey

Selected poems from *Les Fleurs du Mal* are translated with parallel French texts and are designed to be read with pleasure by readers who have no French as well as those who are practised in the French language.

F.W. Leakey was Professor of French in the University of London. As a scholar, critic and teacher he specialised in the work of Baudelaire for 50 years and published a number of books on the poet.

2001 • 153 pages • ISBN 1-871551-10-2

Lines from the Stone Age

Sean Haldane

Reviewing Sean Haldane's 1992 volume *Desire in Belfast*, Robert Nye wrote in *The Times* that "Haldane can be sure of his place among the English poets." This place is not yet a conspicuous one, mainly because his early volumes appeared in Canada and because he has earned his living by other means than literature. Despite this, his poems have always had their circle of readers. The 60 previously unpublished poems of *Lines from the Stone Age* – "lines of longing, terror, pride, lust and pain" – may widen this circle.

2000 • 53 pages • ISBN 1-871551-39-0

Wilderness

Martin Seymour-Smith

This is Martin Seymour-Smith's first publication of his poetry since the mid 1970s. This collection of 36 poems is a fearless account of an inner life of love, frustration, guilt, laughter and the celebration of others. He is best known to the general public as the author of the controversial and bestselling *Hardy* (1994).

1994 • 52 pages • ISBN 1-871551-08-0